Aberdeen Street Names

Aberdeen from Torry Farm, *c.* 1860.

Aberdeen Street Names

Their History, Meaning, and Personal Associations

BY

G. M. FRASER

LIBRARIAN, ABERDEEN PUBLIC LIBRARY

with a new Foreword and a Supplement by

MOIRA HENDERSON

ABERDEENSHIRE CLASSICS

James G. Bisset
12 Upperkirkgate
Aberdeen
1986

Republished from the original 1911 edition
by

James G. Bisset
12 Upperkirkgate
Aberdeen
AB9 1BG

British Library Cataloguing in Publication Data
Fraser, G.M. (George Milne)
Aberdeenshire Street Names — New ed. —
(Aberdeenshire Classics)
1. Street names — Scotland — Aberdeen (Grampian)
I. Title II. Henderson, Moira III. Series
914.12°35°0014 DA890.A2

ISBN: 0–948246–04–9

Printed by Fretwell & Cox Ltd., Keighley, West Yorkshire

The Author

"WE must now regard you as our principal historian". These words were written to G.M. Fraser by Aberdeen's Town Clerk Depute, following the publication of *Aberdeen Street Names* in 1911. To the forty-eight-year-old Public Librarian, such recognition must have seemed the realisation of a dream, for his early circumstances had indicated a totally different way of life and he was certainly no stranger to hard work, disappointment and criticism.

George Milne Fraser was born on 31st October 1862, at the farm of Haddo, Methlick, where his father, Joseph Fraser, was a farm servant. His paternal grandfather was a blacksmith in the village of Gamrie, and his mother, Mary Taylor, was the daughter of a Strichen farm worker. Joseph and Mary were married in 1854, and their movements during the next decade from Strichen to Old Deer, Methlick and Auchterless, reflect the uncertainties of the farm servant's life and the need to provide for a growing family, for George was to be the fourth child in a family of twelve.

By the mid 1860's granite polishing had become an important industry in Aberdeen, and the products of her twenty-four polishing yards were in demand in many different parts of the world in the form of monuments, fountains and decorative architecture. The industry drew much of its workforce from the hinterland, and about 1868 the Fraser family moved to a house in Minister Lane in the

Gilcomston area. It seems that Joseph quickly found work as a labourer with Messrs. J. and J. Ogg of Holburn Street and later of Clayhills, where he was to spend the rest of his working life. Of the schooldays of the six Fraser brothers we have no record, but family tradition says they were of necessity brief, and that George was largely self-educated. Certainly, by 1881 he and two younger brothers, Joe and Alex, were all working as apprentice stonecutters. Joe later became a very popular figure in the granite industry, and from 1905–1914 was General Secretary of the Monumental Branch of the Operative Masons' Union. George, however, was destined to follow a very different career, for an accident in the granite yard cost him an eye and changed his life at a stroke.

In 1887, attracted to a career in journalism, he called on Dr. William Alexander of the *Free Press,* and, as a test of his skills, was asked to write an account of a lecture which was to be given in the Blackfriars Street Hall on the subject of the American poet, Ralph Waldo Emerson. In later years he confessed to having been too shy to take notes during the meeting or to write his report in the newspaper office. It was written instead in the open air, by the gas-light of a tobacconist's window in Hadden Street. Soon after, however, he was invited to join the staff of the *Free Press,* and the next thirteen years saw him develop into a reporter of exceptional accuracy and clarity, with a talent for reviewing and a lasting enthusiasm for local history. His work on the *Free Press* and its sister paper the *Evening Gazette* introduced him to men of influence in local industry, politics, education and church affairs and gave him a substantial knowledge of public movements and events in the whole North-East. An important factor in his success as a journalist was the encouragement given to him by Dr. Alexander and his brother Henry who had succeeded him as Editor, and in an article written in 1922 to mark the Golden Jubilee of the *Free Press*, Mr. Fraser pays tribute to their kindness, their moral principles and their high standards of journalism. Perhaps it is significant that Henry Alexander too had suffered the loss of an eye, and we can imagine that he took a special pleasure in helping to develop the talents and confidence of the young reporter on his staff. In the autumn of 1891 Mr. Fraser married Barbara Morrison Greenlaw, the daughter of an Aberdeen businessman, and their only child, Douglas, was born in September 1892.

Towards the end of 1899 the members of Aberdeen's Public Library Committee received the surprise resignation of their scholarly Librarian, Alexander W. Robertson. He was only fifty-two years old, but now wished to devote his time to study. The search for a successor was launched by the insertion of an advertisement in the local Press and in the leading national literary journals, resulting in thirty-nine applications from as far afield as Manchester, Sussex and even Cairo. Twenty-five of these men were experienced librarians, but the candidates also included a dentist, a tailor, a retired minister and several teachers, for the advertisement had stipulated only that applicants should be under forty-five years of age. A short leet of six was drawn up and a storm of protest erupted in the columns of *The Aberdeen Journal* and of *The Evening Express* when it was found to include the name of George Milne Fraser, journalist. Correspondents writing under such pseudonyms as "One who knows", "Straight" and "Citizen", commented on Mr. Fraser's total lack of library experience and accused the Labour members of the Library Committee of scheming and manipulation. The *Journal* even printed extracts from the testimonials of a rival candidate and concluded its campaign with a thundering editorial in which it denounced the Committee's "misleading and illusory advertisement". Mr. Fraser, however, had many influential supporters, and his seventeen testimonials were supplied by clergymen, lawyers, professors, businessmen and a member of the House of Lords. On the 29th December the Library Committee met to make its decision, and G.M. Fraser was appointed on a final vote of 13 to 7.

And so began a commitment to Aberdeen and its Library which was to last for nearly forty years. His critics were gradually won over, and honest Baillie George Walker, who had been totally opposed to the appointment, was able to write in 1901, "Mr. Fraser has quite justified the opinion of his friends". During his term of office there were many developments in library provision. The Central Library was transformed in 1905 by the addition of a splendid new reading room, and the service was extended to outlying parts of the city through a series of branch reading rooms and delivery stations. Many citizens remember with affection the Juvenile Library in Skene Street which was opened in 1911, while others recall the excitement of the Lending Library's conversion to open access in 1925. One of G.M. Fraser's finest memorials, however, is the Library's Local Collection, for he was responsible for the acquisition of much of its valuable stock. Children were especially encouraged to take an interest in the history of their city, and in 1914 in the Juvenile Library he gave the first of a remarkable series of local history lectures which he was to continue throughout every winter till 1934. Over the years he covered all manner of fascinating subjects, ranging from historical buildings, streets and battles to the name derivations of schools, hills and lochs. Each lecture was attended by some three hundred children, who were later invited to send in essays on the evening's topic. The prizes were works on local history, and some of these volumes are still cherished today in homes throughout the city. Adults too, enjoyed his lectures, and his name appears on the programmes of numerous local associations. He was very proud of being the first public librarian to make a radio broadcast, for on the 30th October 1923 he gave a fifteen-minute talk on *The Castlegate and its associations* from the recently opened Aberdeen Studio in Belmont Street.

Despite all these activities his talents were not lost to journalism, and the familiar initials "G.M.F." give testimony to the authorship of innumerable articles and letters which appeared in local newspapers and in periodicals with a nation-wide circulation. Some of these newspaper articles were later included in his local history books, published mainly by William Smith & Sons of the Bon-Accord Press. *The Green and its story* appeared in 1904, and in the following year *Historical Aberdeen* told the story of the Castlehill, the Snow Church, Woolmanhill and the Guestrow. Popular response encouraged him to contribute a series of articles on a similar theme to the *Evening Gazette* and these were the basis of *Aberdeen Street Names* published in 1911. In later volumes he covered such subjects as the Bridge of Dee, the Mechanics' Institute, the Old Deeside Road and the origins of the Aberdonian. Sadly, in 1912 his wife died and in the dedication of *The Bridge of Dee* he pays tribute to her unfailing encouragement and help. Four years later he re-married, and his bride was Miss Isabella Jane Henderson who had been an assistant in the Library's Reference Department. "Tibby", as he called her, shared many of his interests and was a willing companion on walks and local history excursions.

To a whole generation of Aberdonians G.M. Fraser was a familiar figure as he made his regular daily rounds of the Library departments or walked briskly to and from his home in Hamilton Place. Small, spare and bespectacled, he was usually dressed in grey suit, white shirt and winged collar, though excursions with the Deeside Field Club found him in his holiday attire of "plusfours". His name was known all over the North-East and certainly the audiences at the Beach Pavilion were in no doubt as to his identity when they shouted his name in a chorus to one of Harry Gordon's most popular songs. His successor, Marcus Milne, worked with him for fifteen years and remembers him as a man of habit, rather remote from his staff, but always ready to share his knowledge of Aberdeen places and people. He seems to have had few intimate friends but took pleasure in corresponding with fellow enthusiasts, prominent among whom were P.J. Anderson, the University Librarian, James Cruickshank, the Newhills historian and G. Gordon Jenkins, his collaborator on *The Old Deeside Road*. Always interested in young people, he taught a Bible Class at Rosemount

Church for sixteen years. At the time of his death he was senior elder there and had given years of enthusiastic support to Aberdeen Elders' Union.

G.M. Fraser died on 7th June 1938 at the age of seventy-five. He had been Public Librarian for more than thirty-eight years and shortly before his death he completed a series of evening lectures regularly attended by some 125 adults. In Springbank Cemetery his grave is marked by a modest tombstone and in Rosemount Church his monument takes the form of a memorial window, gifted by his widow, and bearing the text "I have finished the work Thou gavest me to do" (John 17 verse 4). In 1955 Aberdeen's first post-war permanent branch library was opened at Northfield and named the *G.M. Fraser Branch Library* in his honour. Mrs. Isabella Fraser died in August 1953 in her eightieth year.

August, 1986 Moira Henderson

INTRODUCTORY

THE study of the street names of our Scottish and English burghs has been so much neglected that we need to be reminded a little of its scope and interest.

Early street names are all valuable, first, as illustrating historical and early topographical conditions. We can scarcely look into the written history of any of our older towns without seeing how much historical interest lies imbedded in the street names that are only incidentally mentioned; and without remarking, too, how indifferent the writers almost always are to the helpful and suggestive matter thus lying ready to their hand in the pages of their own books. The case of Aberdeen is no exception. Although its story has been written frequently, and in several instances in historical works of high quality, the early street names have not been seriously looked upon hitherto as of special historical or topographical significance.

And, secondly, those early street names are in themselves well worthy of accurate study, for, rightly understood, they are always the centre of a variety of most suggestive historical and personal interests. One might safely say that it is impossible for a street name more than fifty years old to be uninteresting, and if that be so, we can easily see how rich in historical and personal interest are the street names that are as old as a burgh itself, and may have remained the only unchanging features in a burgh throughout centuries of its history. This book has been written in order that as far as Aberdeen is concerned these things may be put on record once for all; also, to help, if possible, to a more enlightened interest in the whole subject of our historical possessions.

It should be said that this volume is based on the series of articles contributed by the present writer to the *Aberdeen Evening Gazette* in the summer of 1909. To the proprietors of the same acknowledgment is due for permission to utilise these articles for the this volume.

G. M. FRASER.

99, HAMILTON PLACE,
February, 1911.

CONTENTS

Contents

Contents

ILLUSTRATIONS

Aberdeen Street Names

CHAPTER I

THE ORIGIN OF STREET NAMES IN SCOTTISH TOWNS: FORMAL NAMING COMPARATIVELY RECENT: COMMENCEMENT OF THE PRACTICE IN ABERDEEN: THE POLICE COMMISSIONERS AND THEIR WORK: THE CASTLEGATE: THE USE OF "GATE" IN STREET NAMES: SOME HISTORICAL ASSOCIATIONS.

IN these chapters dealing with the street names of Aberdeen the origin and meaning of the names will be, of course, the main topic. Where, however, a street has played some special part in civic history, through its name or otherwise, or has been the residence of some person noteworthy in the annals of the city, we shall not hesitate to go a little into historical and personal affairs. The whole range of the burgh's history since the twelfth century is marked by a variety of the most interesting events, and as we shall have to cover the whole period, more or less, in dealing with the street names, we shall now and again touch upon those events both to illustrate our subject, and to keep in touch with living things.

One other preliminary remark may be allowed in order to point out what, so far as I know, is the earliest mention of a particular street (and the earliest record of what would now be termed a street name) in Aberdeen. It occurs in the Chartulary of the Abbey of Arbroath. About the year 1212, nearly two centuries before our set of the Burgh Register begins, the Abbot and Convent of Arbroath granted a charter to Gilbert Stute, burgess of Aberdeen, and Emma, his spouse, entitling them to a piece of ground as follows :—

> "tota terra nostra quam habemus in burgo de Abirdene videlicet a ponte per quem sit transitus a vico fraxini usque ad ecclesiam beati Nicholai qui vocatur Kirkebrig et quae sita est inter duos rivulos qui bifurcantur a predicto ponte usque ad domum quae fuit Henrici Molendinarii."*

[All that piece of land which we hold in the burgh of Aberdeen, namely, from the bridge by which the crossing is made from the Vicus Fraxini—the Road of the Ash Tree—to the Church of St. Nicholas, which is called the Kirk-brig, and which is situated between the two streams, which are divided by the said bridge, to the house that was the house of Henry the Miller].

It is not very easy to say precisely where this Vicus Fraxini, or Road of the Ash Tree, was situated. Keeping in view, however, that the streams mentioned flowed from the Loch past the east end of St. Nicholas

*Registrum de Aberbrothoc, I., p. 98. In Dr. Joseph Robertson's day the earliest known street names were the Green, 1273, and the Castlegate and Gallowgate, by 1350. See "Book of Bon-Accord," p. 103. In the present work, however, we shall find ourselves in familiar touch with the early streets before these dates.

Church to the river estuary, I think we may reasonably conclude that the bridge stood to the eastward of the Church. If that be so, the Road of the Ash Tree could only be what became—and is still—known as the Netherkirkgate, for it is the only street that could be carried past the shoulder of St. Katherine's Hill (not yet named in 1212), and it ran down to the Flour Mill Burn, opposite the Church, and sixty or seventy yards below where the mill stood for centuries. In that case we get a glimpse through this old charter into a most interesting state of things. It must be that the Castle was built about this time. But there were as yet no houses in all that now over-crowded district that lies northward of the lower end of Union Street—no Broadgate even, or Gallowgate, or Upperkirkgate, and no Schoolhill, for it is half a century after this date before we find the earliest meagre reference to the Grammar School. It is all more or less commonty sloping towards the hollow of the loch, and the Netherkirkgate itself is merely a country lane, leading through ash trees to the Church. What would we not give for an authentic picture of this Aberdeen of 1212. The town, we must bear in mind, was a fully organised burgh by that time, holding charters from the king, and using a common seal, with which this charter to Gilbert Stute and his wife is sealed in due form. But the civic life of the burgh, gathered round the old tolbooth near the shore, must have been a very simple and quiet thing, and we may be thankful to have even this glance at affairs through the ancient Road of the Ash Tree, the first street name to appear to us through the mists.*

At the very outset, too, we must note that although we are dealing only with the street names of Aberdeen, our subject is a little wider than that. The conditions that gave rise to street names in one Scottish town were just the same, on the whole, as in other Scottish towns of the same period. So you find Castlegates, and Cowgates, and High Streets, and Gallowgates, and Causewayends, and Vennels in most of our older burghs, and the names arose in the different towns in precisely the same way, and from the same cause. And the cause was simply the natural necessity that arose for distinguishing in some way the different roads in a burgh, when these burghs began to grow to any extent. In point of fact, our early street names were not really names at all, but natural descriptions of the various thoroughfares. That is to say, in the early days our streets had no names, as such; they were simply spoken of in a descriptive way as the Ship-raw, the Causeway-end, the Cow-gait, the Dubby Raw, the Broad-gait, and so on, and in due time this descriptive designation remained as the name of the street.

*Incidentally, this charter of 1212 advances our knowledge in another way. As above-said, the charter is sealed with "the common seal of the Burgh of Abirden." Hitherto, the earliest authentic notice of the use of a seal by the burgh of Aberdeen is in a charter of 1271, in the Advocates' Library in Edinburgh. See Cruickshank's "Armorial Ensigns of the Burgh of Aberdeen," p. 5. The foregoing advances our knowledge by sixty years.

Following upon this we must keep in mind that the formal, official naming of our streets is a comparatively recent practice. In Aberdeen, it is not older, I think, than about a century and a half. We shall see, as we go on, what streets have the distinction of first formally receiving names, but prior to about 1750 the burgh streets were spoken of in a purely descriptive way, according to their character, or situation, or use. This, of course, is how it happens that all our older street names in Aberdeen are so strictly descriptive, and being descriptive are so valuable now when original conditions have so greatly changed. In many cases these old street names preserve for us the memory of places and customs and social conditions which, but for them, would have slipped long ago from the public recollection.*

Although new streets began to be named in an official way in Aberdeen about the middle of the eighteenth century, it was not till fifty years later that the matter was put upon a clear and proper basis. Between about 1750 and the end of that century such street names as were given were applied by the Town Council, or by private feuars themselves, in a more or less haphazard way. By the Aberdeen Police Act of 1795, however, a new ruling authority was brought into being, namely, the Police Commissioners, who

*Very good examples of this are the still existing street names in Aberdeen—the Spital, where there is no Hospital now, the Woolmanhill, where there is now no wool market, the Port Hill, where there is no port, or gateway, and so on. Other examples of the same thing will emerge as we go on.

were charged with the care of the streets and waterworks, and to whom a really vast improvement in the social conditions of Aberdeen was due, especially during the first quarter of last century. The new Commissioners were full of zeal. They were guided mainly by one man, John Ewen, the reputed author of the well-known song, "The Boatie Rows," a busybody to the backbone, whose curio shop in the Castlegate was a centre of political and municipal discussion for years. But he was an enlightened man in many ways, and it was to him, more than to any other single person, that the Police Act of 1795 was due, and through it his work endures to this day.*

One of the clauses of the Police Act of 1795 provided for the systematic naming of the streets and the numbering of the houses, and as all the really efficient work in this way followed on this Act, it may be of interest to quote the exact terms of the clause :—

> "And be it further enacted that the said [Police] Commissioners shall and may cause to be painted, engraved, or described, on stone, or otherwise, and to be affixed on a conspicuous part of one or more house or houses, building or buildings, at or near each end, corner, or entrance to the said streets, lanes, or other passages of the said City of Aberdeen, the name by which they are respectively to be called or known; and may also

*John Ewen died 21st October, 1821, leaving his fortune of about £14,000 to found in his native town of Montrose an institution after the pattern of Gordon's Hospital, Aberdeen. The Court of Session found that a daughter of his had a prior claim, and set aside the will in her favour. See particularly, *Aberdeen Journal*, 5th February, 1822, and 12th February, 1823.

cause every house, shop, or warehouse in the said streets lanes, or passages, at the expense of the possessors, to be marked or numbered in such manner as they shall judge most proper for distinguishing the same; and if any person or persons shall wilfully or maliciously destroy, pull down, obliterate, or deface any such name, description marks, or numbers, or any part thereof, or cause or procure the same to be done, every person so offending shall, for every offence, forfeit and pay the sum of twenty shillings sterling."*

It cannot be said that the effect of this clause in the Act of 1795 was either immediate or magical. In point of fact, the numbering of the houses was not systematically and fully carried out for years after that time, and with regard to the naming of the streets we find a very curious complaint brought before the Police Commissioners by John Ewen himself—vice-chairman of the body—as late as 1809. Thus—

"25 September, 1809—The Treasurer laid before the Board an account from George Gordon, painter, for painting the names on the different streets and lanes of this city, which, he says, his father John Gordon, had given over to him, as from certain circumstances in his father's situation he was unable to accomplish himself. The Treasurer was directed to examine the account and, if correct, settle it.

"Mr. Ewen stated to the Board that he had had several applications from different people in consequence of errors committed by the painter in painting on improper names in several of the streets and lanes, and in particular

*Aberdeen Police Act, 1795. This Act was to endure for a period of only twenty years, but it was renewed in 1818, again through the initiative of John Ewen, with the above clause as it stood.

Custom House Lane, instead of Shore Lane, Hall Street, instead of Park Street, and Donald Street instead of Loch Street, all of which had been so painted without any authority. The Commissioners, wishing to depart as little as possible from old names, unless where there was evident propriety in the change, had sanctioned the change to Custom House Lane of Shore Lane, of what was Park Road to Park Street, and the passage from Drum's Lane, crossing George Street and Harriet Street at right angles, to Loch Street." *

The public of Aberdeen, as of other towns, Scottish and English, may be glad that this policy of departing as little as possible from old names was so largely followed when the formal naming of streets began to engage special attention. Otherwise, these towns would be much less interesting in some ways than they are.

Keeping these general points in view, then, we pass to the consideration of particular street names. We begin with one of the very oldest, and certainly one of the most familiar throughout the history of the burgh, namely, the Castlegate. How old that name is no one can tell precisely. We know it for six hundred and forty years, from 1272, our first record of the existence of the Castle of Aberdeen, and it probably goes back at least half a century earlier still, for it is certainly as old as the Castle itself, which stood on the adjoining Castlehill. But this we do know with certainty that, apart from its incidental designation as the "Market-gate," this is the only name that the street has ever borne. Before the period of the Castle, the little trading and fishing town by the shore, that Aberdeen

* Register of Aberdeen Police Commissioners, II., folio 25.

John Ewen,

Police Commissioner; one of the Authors of Police Act, 1795.

From a miniature by A. Robertson.

then was, had no need of a street on the hill-top (apart from a convenient road to the Church). And we can easily imagine that when permission was obtained from King Robert III., in 1394, to erect a new town-house or tolbooth, in place of the old tolbooth by the water side, and when it was decided to build it in the Castlegate, the Solomons of the little burgh would shake their wise heads and say a great mistake was being made—the new site was too far from the business centre of the town!*

The meaning of the name "Castlegate" is fairly obvious. Note, however, that the word "gate" in the name has nothing whatever to do with an opening or entrance through a wall, or enclosure. It is the old Scots word "gait"—spelt "gait" in Scotland from the fourteenth century—meaning a road, or way. "Down that gait," meaning down that road or way, used to be a very common Scots phrase, and Scots poetry often makes use of the word in this interesting and picturesque sense. The "Castlegait," then, is just the Castle Road, a purely descriptive designation, properly enough rendered in our present-day usage by its present name of Castle Street. And this in almost every instance is the real meaning of the word "gate" in the street names of all our Scottish burghs, and of

*This plea was urged in the course of a strong public agitation, in 1819, against placing the Music Hall so far west as the present site, near Silver Street. The same thing was said a few years ago against erecting the new Post Office on its present site in Crown Street. The plea will probably always be urged in any growing community against any scheme that is at all in advance of the public convenience of the time.

certain towns in the north of England.* From this it will be seen that we have now a key to the meaning of several other old street names in Aberdeen. The name of the "Gallowgate" had nothing to do with the old city gate that was situated there, but simply described the Gallow Road, that is, the way or "gait" to the Gallow Hill, by which the meaner sort of offenders were led to the scaffold. "Via Furcarum" is the frequent designation of the street in the old Latin charters, and this being translated "Thief Gait" not only describes its use as the Gallow-gait, but is the actual name by which it was often described in familiar speech among the townsfolk.

This Castlegate of ours has had the very closest association with the burghal life of Aberdeen through all these six hundred years. We have just said that it has sometimes been spoken of as the "Market-gate." It is not so often given in that English form, however, as in the corresponding Latin term "forum," or "foro" —for it must be remembered that our oldest and most valuable charters are written in Latin, and that is not altogether a disadvantage, because it often helps us to the precise meaning that was attached to an ordinary name the form of which may have become so changed in the English spelling that we should scarcely be able to recognise the original.†

*This, of course, is quite different from such cases as Bishopsgate, Cripplegate, Ludgate, Newgate, etc., in London. These are the names of actual gateways.

†This is specially noticeable in the name of the Ghaist-Row, for many years (and still) erroneously spelt Guestrow, as we shall see more fully in due time.

But the use of the term "forum," or market-place, to designate the Castlegate, guides us to the interesting fact that the early kings of Scotland held property in the Castlegate. In the register of the Abbey of Arbroath there is a charter granted in 1219 by Robert, brother of King Alexander II., in which he specifies certain properties granted, but particularly reserves the "hostilagium which is in my toft opposite the forum in Aberdeen, which I granted to King Alexander, my brother."* In those days the King's "hostilagium" was a house to be found in every Scottish burgh. It seems to have been a sort of warehouse, or bond, for the goods of outside merchants, not "freemen" of the burgh, on which special duties had to be paid before the goods could be exposed for sale in the burgh market.†

There was also a different kind of "hostilagium," or "hostillarie," in the principal towns, maintained for the use of travellers, but these were inns, or "hostelries," as we now say, which were held bound to have in hand, at all times, "bread and aill, and all uther fude, alsweil for horse as men, for reasonabil price," as says an old Scots Act of Parliament of James I, of date 26th May, 1424. But this other kind of "hostillarie" stood in Aberdeen in the Netherkirkgate, which was just the right place then, being the main route in the line of the Green and the

*Registrum de Aberbrothoc, I., p. 195.

†At one time the term "hostilagium" seems to have meant the rent which these outside merchants paid for such store-houses, but as often happens, it came to be applied to the house itself.

Windmill Brae, of all travellers to and from the south.*

In those old days one other notable official building stood in the Castlegate, and that was the court-house of the Justiciary of Scotland, Comyn, the Earl of Buchan, whose son was such an inveterate enemy of Robert the Bruce. He was frequently in Aberdeen in his capacity of Justiciar, and sat "near the Castle of Aberdeen, in the place which is called Castlesyd."† That, we may take it, was somewhere about the east-end of the Castlegate, under the shadow of the fortress on the Castlehill, which was destroyed by the Bruce party about 1308.

One would like to linger over the associations—the literary associations particularly—of the Castlegate, the most historic of our burgh streets. But that is not possible. We can only recall that it was in the north side of the Castlegate that Edward Raban, Aberdeen's first printer, set up his printing-press in 1622. Since that time there has nearly always been a printer in the street, and the publications that have come from

*In 1276, the Abbot of Arbroath granted to Walter de Melville in Aberdeen, a toft of land near the Castle, and two "perticatas" or poles, of land in the Netherkirkgate, which the Abbots had previously received in charter from King William, and the return that Walter de Melville had to make was twelve pennies annually at Pentecost, and in his "hostilagium" to provide the monks and their retinue as often as they came to Aberdeen with shelter, fire, candle-light, salt, and bed-clothing, after the practice of very ancient times. See *Reg. de Aberb.*, I., 325.

†Registrum de Aberbrothoc, I., p. 164.

Castlegate presses cover the most varied subjects. It was from the old printing-house in the Castlegate that James Chalmers, the last printer who enjoyed the monopoly of Town's Printer in Aberdeen, first published the *Aberdeen Journal* in 1748, which still appears, the oldest newspaper in Scotland. We must not forget, too, that the most noted private Reading Room and Library that the town ever possessed was situated in the Castlegate. This was the "Athenæum," started by Provost Brown, father of the late Rev. Principal Brown, away back in the opening years of last century. It was carried on for nearly twenty years in Castle Street, about where the cleared Exchequer Row area is, until it was removed in 1822 into the fine new structure built by Provost Brown, at the west end of the Castlegate. That building then took the name of the Athenæum, and under a different use is so designated to this day.

CHAPTER II

THE MAKING OF "SLUM" PROPERTY: NAMES OF CASTLEGATE CLOSES: BURNETT'S CLOSE: THE "SHELLY" CLOSE: FRANCIS PEACOCK AND PEACOCK'S CLOSE: THE TOWN COUNCIL AND THE DANCING MASTER.

BEFORE leaving the Castlegate we ought to touch on the names of one or two of the old courts and closes there. It will be noted that a very large number of these closes, striking off the older streets of the town, bear personal names, those of feuars or proprietors of the ground. They nearly all date from the second half of the eighteenth century, when it was supposed that the town could not possibly be extended beyond its then limits. Accordingly, the only way to provide accommodation for the increasing population, which began to mount up after the Jacobite Rebellion of 1745, was to use up the gardens along both sides of these older streets—the Castlegate, Shiprow, Gallowgate, Guestrow, and so on. Lanes and closes were carried through these back gardens, entered, in many cases, through "pends" in order to save the front houses as much as possible, and it is from this cause that the ancient garden ground disappeared, and the congested properties arose which we know so well to-day by the name of the "slums" of the city. It was a wretched practice from every point of view, from which Aberdeen still suffers, and it indicates that the narrow cramped condition of the little burgh was reflected in the narrow, short-sighted views of the then rulers of the town. The names of certain of these closes, however, recall personal and other associations which closely touch the history of the community.

Of these Castlegate courts, Burnett's Close used to be rather too well known. It has now disappeared as part of the "Exchequer Row area" which Professor Matthew Hay, the Medical Officer of Health, got the Town Council to schedule for demolition in 1896. The Burnett whose name was commemorated in the name of the close was Robert Burnett of Elrick, a merchant and burgess of Aberdeen. Up till fourteen years ago his house stood at the inner end of the close. Above the door was the coat of arms, beautifully carved in stone, of Robert Burnett and his wife;* and another block told the actual date of the building, *viz.*, "1669." Burnett of Elrick was, no doubt, a very worthy citizen, but when his house was demolished fourteen years ago a very curious secret passage was discovered, carefully built and concealed, which ran from the cellars of his house in Burnett's Close to the shore, offering the suggestion that he was not above doing a little illicit trading with the Continent. †

*The coat of arms is now preserved in the Town House.

† In the early years of last century this house was a rather noted tavern, known as Affleck's Tavern. In 1841 it was

His successor, but one, in this house was Andrew Burnett of Elrick, a Baillie of the city, who married Marjory Johnston, daughter of Sir John Johnston of Caskieben (the property now known as Keith-hall and occupied by Lord Kintore). It was this Baillie Burnett who built, as a country house, in 1783, the house of Belmont, near Kittybrewster, known at first as Bushey Bank. He died in his house in Burnett's Close in February, 1806, in his 86th year, and like his predecessor, Robert Burnett of Elrick, lies in the Burnett vault by the west wall of St. Nicholas Churchyard.

I am sure it will interest many to know that it was in Burnett's Close that Robert Seaton, whose admirable Aberdeen views are so well known, had his studio and art classes. Here is a copy of his "card," issued in April, 1807:—

> "R. Seaton begs leave to announce to his late pupils and the ladies and gentlemen of Aberdeen and its vicinity that he proposes, on Monday, 20th of April, to recommence teaching his public classes, at a large and well-lighted room in Burnett's Close, at the house of Mr. Gartley, watchmaker. Terms as before—£1 1s per

advertised for sale as having been "formerly occupied by the late John Affleck, and latterly by his widow, and well known to be the most *recherche* Eating House in the north of Scotland." One of the advantages of the property was said to be a "vaulted cellar attached to the premises," no doubt the vaulted cellar revealed when the house was recently demolished. John Affleck was a brother of Andrew Affleck, Convener of the Trades, a worthy and esteemed citizen.

Broad Street.

Showing the Residence of Lord Byron.

quarter—days and hours of teaching the same as before. Further particulars may be had by inquiry at Mr. Seaton's lodgings, at Mr. Gartley's."*

The adjoining court to Burnett's Close, and also demolished now as part of the condemned Exchequer Row area, was Stronach's Close. It, too, in later years had a very bad reputation, and gave many unhappy cases to the Aberdeen courts of justice, yet it had an interesting historical side as well as the others.

The person who gave his name to this close was Robert Stronach, wright, who owned some houses in the close, and from a curious practice that he had, the close came latterly to have the name of the "Shally" Close. This was a corruption of "Shelly" Close, and the name arose—as John Ramsay tells in his "Aberdoniana"—in this way. "Robert's peculiar fancy was the decoration of his houses with shells stuck on the walls with plaster in various fantastic forms. With this view it was his custom to traverse the sea-beach after storms, and pick up the shells which Ocean in his agony had vomited. These he stowed away in the capacious pockets of a blue great-coat, which it was his comfort to wear on such occasions. His occasional competitors were school-boys rummaging for 'carn tangles,' a marine delicacy suitable for no stomach but theirs, or that of an ostrich. Like one of the soldiers of the conchological Roman Emperor, Robert would return home laden with the spoils of the deep, which in due time figured,

*Two of Seaton's best known Aberdeen views (painted by Nasymth from Seaton's drawings) formerly owned by the late Dean Danson, have this year (1910) been acquired by the Town Council.

painted in various colours, on the walls of his tenements." *

The writer never saw the shells of the "Shelly" Close, but a friend now turning into the seventies remembers the curious decoration very well away back in the first half of last century. Robert Stronach's houses must have had a very grotesque appearance.†

The most interesting of all the Castlegate closes is Peacock's Close. Over its story we may be permitted to linger for a few moments, for Francis Peacock was not only prominent as a dancing master in Aberdeen, but was esteemed in many other ways as a most worthy citizen.

> "Dancing was introduced at Aberdeen (says Kennedy, the annalist) about the beginning of the eighteenth century, a master being appointed by the Magistrates, with a salary of one hundred merks, for the purpose of teaching the young citizens 'manners and good breeding.'"‡

We take it that the burghers of Aberdeen, like people of other places, danced long before the eighteenth century. In 1695, for example, the Town Council prohibited Mr. Batham, dancing master, "from haveing any publict balls of dancing in this place"§ and even that could not have been the

* Selected writings of John Ramsay, p. 264.

† Robert Stronach's gravestone, with its quaint inscription, his own composition, stands in St. Machar Cathedral graveyard, near the south porch.

‡ Annals of Aberdeen, II., p. 138.

§ Council Register, March, 27, 1695.

first of it. Coming to the originator of Peacock's Close, however, we find, in 1742, the Town Council considering an application by many of the principal inhabitants of Aberdeen setting forth "that the town was at great loss for want of a right dancing master to educate their children," and the Council resolved to advertise for a person of that descripton. As a result two candidates were chosen to exhibit their powers, the Magistrates being the official adjudicators on that interesting occasion. So we are told that

> "James Stuart, dancing master in Montrose, and William Troup, dancing master in Aberdeen, did appear within the Trinity Hall of this burgh, in presence of the Magistrates and great number of gentlemen and ladys, and there did give specimen of their qualifications. The meeting agreed that the said James Stuart by farr exceeded the said William Troup, both in his method of teaching his scholars and his own dancing."*

Accordingly, James Stuart from Montrose was preferred. He did not reign long, however, and we can judge of the unfortunate reason from this that when the Town Council felt it necessary to advertise again for a successor to Stuart, in 1746, they resolved to have a person "of a sober, discreet, and moral character." It was in answer to this advertisement that a letter was received from Mr. John Dawney, dancing master, Edinburgh, recommending Mr. Francis Peacock, of that city, as a fit and qualified person; and on February 14, 1747—

> "The Council nominated and presented and hereby nominate and present the said Mr. Francis Peacock to

*Council Register, June 29, and August 12, 1742.

be sole dancing master within this burgh during his good behaviour, and they allow him to take seven shillings sterling monthly for each scholar, besides payment for the musick." *

Thus began a connection which lasted for the long period of sixty years, of a most honourable kind. When he came to Aberdeen Francis Peacock was but twenty-three, but he seems to have almost immediately after his arrival married an Aberdeen young lady, Ellen Forbes (which is unmistakably an Aberdeen name), and in 1749 the young couple had their first daughter, Elizabeth, baptised in St. Paul's Episcopal Church, at the Lochside.†

Soon after coming to Aberdeen Francis Peacock took up his abode and had his dancing school in what was known as the forehouse of a very remarkable building in the Castlegate, the house that had long been the town house of the Earls Marischal, which stood where the top of Marischal Street now is. When that house was about to be cleared away for the making of Marischal Street, Peacock had to move, and on 26th November, 1766, the matter of providing him with a new dancing hall was talked over by the Town Council who were dispossessing him. On that occasion they "remitted to the Magistrates to consider of a proper room for a Public Dancing School to Mr. Francis Peacock, as the one he presently possesses in Marischall's fore-lodging will be taken

* Council Register, January 17, and February 14, 1747.

† See Mr. Emslie Smith's Baptismal Register of St. Paul's Episcopal Chapel. Mis. of New Spalding Club, II., p. 90.

down next spring." * For a time, Peacock seems to have been accommodated in the old Mealmarket buildings, Mealmarket Street, but in due course he found what might be fitly enough termed his resting-place again in the Castlegate. This was in a property long celebrated in Aberdeen as Skipper Scott's tavern, which also had some notable historical associations, for it was in Skipper Scott's house that the Pretender dined when passing through Aberdeen in December, 1715. † A close ran along the back of Skipper Scott's house, and it was this property that was acquired by Francis Peacock, who soon became a man of considerable means—considerable, that is, for the time—and the close has ever since been known as Peacock's Close.

From this point it is unnecessary to follow Peacock and his history in detail. He became a prominent member of the Aberdeen Musical Society, which gave public weekly concerts in the city for many years. He was an artist, and painted miniatures which were much thought of at the time. In 1762 he published a book, "Fifty Favourite Scotch Airs for the Violin," and he published another, "Sketches Relative to Dancing," in 1805, when he was over eighty years of age. He was also a composer of music, and on the occasion of the coronation of George III., in 1761, the Magistrates and townspeople of Aberdeen gathered in the hall of Marischal College when an anthem composed by Francis Peacock was performed by the gentlemen

* Council Register, LXIII., fol. 66-7.

† A Short Memorandum, p. 2.

of the Musical Society.* As time went on, Peacock built a country house away out near Fountainha', which he named Villa Franca, and many people will still remember it, a yellow stucco-covered house, only demolished in very recent years on the feuing of Hamilton Place West.† He died on June 26, 1807, in his 84th year, very greatly esteemed by the whole community; and as he was personally associated with many worthy movements in his lifetime, he left much of his means to be distributed among the institutions of the town after his death.

The only public memorial of Francis Peacock is the name of this Castlegate close. But that was not always the case. In 1814 the Town Council granted permission to the representatives of Francis Peacock to erect a tablet to his memory in Drum's Aisle, in St. Nicholas Church, on payment of five guineas. What has become of that tablet? Perhaps it was in the way at the rebuilding of the East Church in 1834, and as it represented a person not very much known, probably, at the time, it may have slipped, uncared for, into the rubbish heap.‡

One last thing about Peacock's Close must be noticed. The evil name it has had among the

***Aberdeen Journal*, 1761; reproduced in Turreff's Antiquarian Gleanings, p. 264.

†The modern house built on the site, No. 156 Hamilton Place, still carries on the name, Villa Franca.

‡Peacock's portrait was painted by James Wales, a well-known Aberdeen artist at that time, who was befriended by him. Unfortunately, it has disappeared.

streets of the town is no new thing. In 1850, a petition was presented to the Police Commissioners of Aberdeen, by the feuars and proprietors—"The petitioners prayed the Board to alter the present name of the close, which had fallen into such disrepute that the very name was sufficient to deter many respectable parties from taking houses in that quarter." For some good reason the Board declined to make the change.

Peacock's Close will soon, probably, be a thing of the past. Along the east side of it runs St. Peter's Roman Catholic Chapel—for the better protection of which Priest Gordon was allowed, in 1814, to make some minor improvements in the close, at his own expense. Along the other side of Peacock's Close the old crowded tenements are nearly all abandoned, and the properties will, in due time, be pulled down. The oldest house has had some interesting features in its day. It had the distinction of a flag-staff, and an underground passage, not to speak of the oak panelling of its rooms, much of which has been removed recently to decorate a castellated mansion-house in Aberdeenshire. Even historical interest can not regret the clearance that must soon obliterate a street name that has continued the memory of this most worthy citizen to our own day.

CHAPTER III

JUSTICE STREET AND ITS NEIGHBOURHOOD: AN ANCIENT ROAD TO THE HEADING HILL: THE JUSTICE PORT: THE REMOVAL OF THE ANCIENT GATEWAY: PARK STREET: CONSTITUTION STREET: THE "BOOL" ROAD: WALES STREET.

WE have now dealt with the names of the Castlegate and certain of its more noted courts and closes. At the north-east corner, we strike off the Castlegate by another well-known thoroughfare, namely, Justice Street. Up till very recent days—perhaps still, sometimes—Justice Street was known familiarly in the neighbourhood as "The Port," and that is fully more interesting than the proper name, for it shows the persistence of the old correct expression as applied to the most familiar of the old city ports, or gates. But of that, more presently.

It is sometimes said that Justice Street takes its name from the circumstance that culprits were led through this street to the neighbouring Heading Hill, a place of execution from early times. Sometimes, too, it is suggested that as the Justiciar passed to hold court on the hill this also tended to fix the designation of the street. Perhaps here we ought to explain the street did not then terminate where it does now, on touching Commerce Street, but turned to the right,

West Port, St. Andrews.

(Showing, in the absence of any description or sketch of the Aberdeen Ports, a Scottish Port of the best class).

between the Castlehill and the Heading Hill, leading round the last-named height.*

With regard to this view of the name of Justice Street, the reader must have been struck by one thing. We have seen that all the oldest street names are strictly descriptive. But justice is a very abstract quality, and it seems strange that our forefathers, who were a simple, plain folk, should have made an exception in the name of this street. If it had been called the "Heading" Road, or the "Thieves' Road," or something of that kind, one could have understood it, but "Justice" Street, as a mere street name, seems just a little too advanced for, say, the twelfth or the thirteenth century.

In point of fact, I do not think it was ever called Justice Street until nearly our own time. I have never come across an early charter relating to this street, and my present belief is that there were no houses outside the Justice Port at all until about the seventeenth century, and consequently there was really no "Justice Street," properly so called up to that time. No doubt, a road, as already said, led from the Justice Port round to the Heading Hill, but I cannot think that as early even as the fifteenth century it was ever called the Justice Street.†

* The old direction of Justice Street is very well shown in the map of the crofts appended to Mr. P. J. Anderson's Charters and other Writs illustrating the History of Aberdeen.

† It is curious to note that in John Smith's "Plan of the City of Aberdeen," 1810, the portion of the street from the Castlegate to Park Street is named *Justice Port*, and the con-

This brings us, then, to say a few words on the Justice Port itself. The Justice Port—named from the French *la porte*, a gate or gateway—was one of the six city gates of Aberdeen, the other five being the Futty Port at the top of the Futty Wynd, the Shiprow Port, the Netherkirkgate and Upperkirkgate Ports, and the Gallowgate Port, which stood at the Port-hill. These ports, or gateways, were the chief defence of Aberdeen against either warlike enemy or the plague, and when they were closed the little town was shut off from the outside world.

The precise date of construction of the city ports it seems impossible to determine. Certainly, most of them appear to have been erected prior to 1434, because in an entry of that year in the Council Register it is enacted—

> "That na man na woman pas out of the portis to by anything quhil (till) it be brocht on the market, under the payn of ane unlaw and escheat (forfeiture) of the thing bocht." *

tinuation in line of what is now Commerce Street is named *Justice Street.* There was evidently a doubt on the subject even at that time.

*Extracts from the Council Register, Spalding Club, I., p. 391. In passing this enactment against "forestallers," as they were termed, the Aberdeen Council were merely putting into force locally what the Scots Parliament had decreed for the whole country. It was intended to protect the community from what would now be termed "corners." Thus the Parliament of David II.—"Na man dwelland within nor without [any] burgh sal in the market day passe forth of the Portes of the burgh to

If this can be taken to refer to the ports generally, then we know that the Justice Port was the last to be erected, because in the same Council Register we are told that on September 13, 1440, one David Farquharson was admitted a free burgess and guild brother, "and in respect of his admission as a freeman he gave to the building of the port in the east end of the Castlegate, five merks."* Now, it is very clear from the foregoing that when the port was built it was not in any "street" leading out of the Castlegate, but at the verge of the Castlegate itself; and this, I believe, remained the limit of the town at that part for at least a century and a half, probably more. We know, at anyrate, that when the Laird of Balquhain with fifty horsemen made a raid on Aberdeen, he rode up to the Justice Port, but "gat na entranss" to the town.† Soon after its erection in 1440, however, the port began to be termed the Justice Port, partly, no doubt, from the fact that it did lead to the Heading Hill, as already said, and partly because upon it were "spiked" the dismembered limbs of

buy anything, before that thing be brocht within the Ports of the burgh : And he quha is convict heiranent sal pay ane unlaw of aucht shilling." Skene, Regiam Majestatem, ff. 128, etc.

*Council Register, Sp. Club, I., p. 395. A century and a half later, when the Justice Port had fallen into great disrepair, the Council ordered forty merks to be paid to Mr. John Kennedy, Town Clerk, by the Dean of Guild for rebuilding it. Council Register, XXXII., fol. 272.

†Book of Bon-Accord, p. 224.

noted persons who had suffered at the hands of justice.

Of the further detail history of the Justice Port we cannot now speak. A foolish story has been often repeated that the left foot of Wallace was sent to be set up in Aberdeen, the idea being that it was spiked on the Justice Port, but it will be seen that the Justice Port was not built for nearly a century and a half after Wallace's execution; and as a matter of fact, none of the patriot's limbs was sent to Aberdeen.* The fate of the Justice Port, and the other ports of the town, was decreed in 1769, when the Town Council, considering that these structures were great obstructions to carriages of all kinds, "of which repeated complaints have been made," instructed that the Justice Port and the Gallowgate Port should be immediately cleared away, and that inquiries should be made with the view of others of the Ports being dealt with in the same way.† For some reason this instruction of the Council was not carried out, and the Justice Port stood for twenty years more.

It is worth while noting specially the demolition of the historic old port, for the record has never previously been made public, and it is the key to the removal of them all. It is from the record of a meeting of the Town Council on June 17, 1787:—

* The official record of Wallace's sentence and execution makes this absolutely clear. The four places to which the limbs were sent were Newcastle, Berwick, Stirling, and Perth. The head was placed on London Bridge. See the sentence of 25th August, 1305, in Chronicles of the Reigns of Edward I. and Edward II., vol. I., p. 142.

† Council Register, LXIII., fol. 119.

"The said day, the Council having heard and considered a petition from John Beattie, mason in Aberdeen, representing that he had been stopt sometime ago in the repairing of the outer stair of a house belonging to him at the Justice Port, on the south side of the street, as being an incroachment on the High Street; that as the Port wall was the west gavel of the said house—if the Council would allow the petitioner to take down and rebuild the same he would put the said stair within the house, and pay £3 sterling for the materials of the Port wall; or if more agreeable, the petitioner would willingly agree to give off on such terms as should be thought reasonable by the Magistrates, two feet all along the front of his house in order to widen the street as well as the said outer stair, and to take in exchange the old Port wall. Which petition having been considered by the Council, they are unanimously of opinion that the last alternative proposed by the petitioner would be most for the enlargement of the High Street and the benefit of the public, and remitt to Baillie Auldjo, the Master of Mortifications, and the Clerk, as a committee, to settle and adjust with the said John Beattie the subject matter of the said petition upon such terms as they shall think most reasonable and adequate." *

So was the fate of the old Justice Port sealed, in a mean and trivial enough way; and as it was the last of the City Ports to be erected, so it was the last to go. It is to be deplored that while the Ports stood, no one thought it worth his while to either describe or sketch them, so we shall never know exactly the appearance of these old gates of the town. It should be said that long after the stone port, or gateway, was cleared away, the street itself—in official records even—bore

*Council Register, LXV., fol. 184.

the name of Justice Port, hence the familiar use of the latter part of the name down to our own time.

Justice Street leads into Park Street, which is an early nineteenth century change from the older descriptive designation of the Park Road. If I were asked, I could not prove it to a demonstration, but I have no doubt that the "Park" mentioned in the name is the Links, perhaps a particular part of the Links. Old writers often speak of the Links as "a smooth dry field," or as "fields near the sea," and there is really no doubt that in the more northerly Links, perhaps where the rifle ranges are now, we have the "Park," for it was thither that the road led. In 1795, when a camp of Fencibles was pitched in the Old Town Links, a petition was presented to the Magistrates of Aberdeen "praying that the Park Road which leads to the Camp may be repaired."* It was not till the opening years of last century that Park Street became really a town thoroughfare, and it was not completed as an ordinary street, as we know it, till nearly half a century later.

Frederick Street and Princes Street, connecting Park Street with King Street, which were both formed in the opening years of last century, carry on their face the meaning of the names. King Street having just been opened (1803) it was natural that these two subsidiary streets should bear minor royal designations. Others of the same kind, belonging to the same period are Queen Street, George Street probably,

*Article by Dr. F. Kelly on "The Last Camp at Aberdeen," *Aberdeen Journal*, 24th July, 1908.

Prince Regent Street, and doubtless Charlotte Street. Neither Frederick Street nor Princes Street ever took a high place in public esteem. Here is the opinion of an artistic correspondent writing to an Aberdeen newspaper in 1807, immediately after the streets he criticises were constructed :

> "Gordon Street (which, by the way, is in a delightful situation) and Chapel Street, made up of shreds and patches, with others, exhibit proofs of this desultory style of buildings, and unnecessary dereliction of regularity and neatness. Even Frederick Street, notwithstanding its high-sounding name, is not entitled to unqualified praise, and Princes Street is most unhappily named, unless it be in compliment to the Prince of Darkness"

The name of Constitution Street shows how much attention was being paid a century ago, in the towns of Scotland, to political affairs. In itself, this street name conveys no meaning ; for an explanation we must go to general history. The street was constructed, in 1807, as a convenient means of access from the Park Road, across the Canal, to the Links. It was made partly on the piece of ground known from ancient days by the name of "Fill-the-Cap," as witness this public intimation in the newspapers of the day :

> "To be feued—The building areas on both sides of a new street, 30 feet wide, which is now made out through the ground of Fill-the-Cap from the Park Road to the Canal Bank, and forming the best and readiest communication with the Links." *

* *Aberdeen Journal*, 8th April, 1807. See also Records of Marischal College (New Sp. Club) for details of feuing of the ground. The meaning of the name "Fill-the-Cap" has been discussed, but so far without any satisfactory result.

For residential purposes the new street was never carried further eastward than the Canal. It was known for a short time as Park Place. About that time, however, it happened that the Town Council and other public bodies in Aberdeen, as in other towns, were enthusiastically passing addresses to George III. for his rejection of the proposals for the political emancipation of Roman Catholics, and—in the words of the resolution passed at a public meeting of citizens in January, 1808—for his "firm determination to support our happy Constitution." It was considered the proper thing to perpetuate the memory of that episode in Aberdeen by giving the name "Constitution" to the new street at Fill-the-Cap. It is amusing now to think that the principal institution in the street, since the year of the Reform Bill, has been a seminary of that very Roman Catholic Church whose repression the street name was intended to celebrate.

The Bowl Road was a street name in the same quarter very familiar to our forefathers. It was applied for centuries to the street now known as Albion Street, which leads eastward from Park Street to the Links. It was long a main thoroughfare leading out of Aberdeen to the north, and through all the troublous times in the middle of the seventeenth century, when Aberdeen was so often raided by both sides in the national struggle, it was by way of the "Bool" Road that the troops repeatedly took their departure—to the relief of the sorely oppressed burghers. In early charters the street is designated the "Boul-get," which is the

"Boul-gait," and that, as we have seen from our discussion of "Castlegate," means precisely the Boul Road.* The proper form of the old name, however, is "Bowl Road," a strictly descriptive name, meaning that the road led to the public bowling-green at the Links. Parson Gordon, writing in 1661, tells us of it in describing the Links:

> "The Lynkis extend themselves almost betwixt the two rivers of Done and Dee. Heer the inhabitants recreat themselves with several kynds of exercises, such as foot-ball, goffe, bowling, and archerie." †

We find from an old map by Gregory Sharpe, of 1732, that at that date the ancient butts and public bowling-green still occupied the ground near the east end of the Bowl Road. History repeated itself in 1842 when a public bowling-green was opened near the Broad Hill, but by that time the name of the Bowl Road had been changed. In 1830 the proprietors petitioned the Police Commissioners, who had charge of the streets and water-works, to change the name of the Bowl Road to Albion Street, in the vain

* Part of the property granted by Sir Alexander Hay of Seaton for the upkeep of the Bridge of Don, in 1605, was the rent of lands "lying between the public road called the Boulget," etc. Kennedy's Annals I., p. 421. We have the name also in a document of date 1531, in William Crynne's statement of his lands in Futty, which included certain lands lying near "Ye Boulgate." Registrum Epis. Aberdonensis, I., 399.

† Description of Both Touns, p. 18. See also the "Description of Aberdeenshire," by Sir Samuel Forbes of Foveran, in the Sp. Club "Collections," p. 47, for a curious description of the bowling-ground.

expectation that a mere change of name could change the character of a street. The Commissioners agreed, and the old descriptive name, which had at least historical interest, ceased to be officially used.

The name of Wales Street, which adjoins, and runs parallel to Albion Street, is very puzzling. In one Plan of Aberdeen, which forms the frontispiece to the first volume of Walter Thom's rather poor "History" of the city (1811), the name is given as Well Street, and when one remembers that a public well was situated near the top of this street the suggestion is sure to arise that here we have the meaning of the name. This would be clearly wrong, however, since in John Smith's earlier "Plan," of 1810, the name is plainly set down as Wales Street. Then, again, one wonders if the name had any association with James Wales, a well known Aberdeen artist who died about the time the street was formed, in the opening years of last century. Probably not. My own present view is that the name is geographical, although why the name of the Principality should be applied to an east end street in Aberdeen is difficult to explain. But the fact that the feuars of the Bowl Road, in 1830, changed the name of that road to Albion Street, after England, seems to show that they took the suggestion from the adjoining Wales Street, and were willing, with such an honourable name, to extend the geographical idea.

Aberdeen, like most old Scottish towns, had a Cowgate until very recently. It was not so much a street—latterly, at all events—as a mere passage, a "vennel," leading from Justice Street behind the Barracks towards Commerce Street. Whenever we find a Cowgate, we are certain to find a common grazing ground in the neighbourhood. It is so in this case. In the old days a grassy flat, well known as the "Green Meadow," lay between the Castlehill and Futty, and was sufficiently distinctive in the seventeenth century to be specifically mentioned in the great Charter granted by Charles I., in 1638, confirming to Aberdeen all the privileges granted to the burgh by his predecessors. We need be in no doubt that the Cowgate got its name from its use as the "gait," or road, by which the cattle of that part of the town were driven from the Justice Port down to the grazing ground at Futty. As late as the eighteenth century many of the feuars in the Castlegate, Broadgate, the Guestrow, and others of the older streets had their brew-houses and their "byres," and although the use of both the Cowgate and the Green Meadow had passed away, this street name long kept in mind the homely conditions that subsisted in the town in earlier times.

CHAPTER IV

"FOOTDEE"—A CORRUPT NAME: THE TRUE MEANING OF FUTTY: ROYAL AND PATRIOTIC STREET NAMES IN THE DISTRICT: A JACOBITE LEADER AND THE SUGAR-HOUSE: THE STORY OF THE WEIGH-HOUSE; MARISCHAL STREET AND ITS ASSOCIATIONS.

FROM the south-east corner of the Castlegate strikes off Castle Terrace, which occupies very nearly the line of the old Futty Wynd, sometimes called the Futty Gate. Another of the old city ports, or gates, stood here, but it is hardly necessary now to say that the name of Futty Gate, or Gait, had nothing to do with the Futty Port, but simply meant the Futty Road. That was the road that led down to the former fisher town and district of Footdee, before the fish-town was removed, in 1808, from the old site near St. Clement's Church to the present site near the pier.

The absurdity of the name "Footdee" must have occurred to many people. At the first glance—keeping in view that the River Dee issues there—it seems to mean the Foot of the Dee. But a moment's thought is enough to dismiss the idea. Even if we accepted it that the "foot" of a river (if such a thing could be imagined) could stand for its mouth, such a phrase has never been in such popular use as to establish a place-name. In point of fact, the name is an ignorant corruption which culminated in the eighteenth century, and we can trace the process of corruption backwards from that time through the names "Futt Dee," "Footie," "Futty," "Foty," to "Fotin" in the fourteenth century. This takes us then to the site of the old chapel dedicated to St. Fotin, otherwise St. Fotinus, which in the usual way became shortened to Foty. It is rather a beautiful story—told by Bishop Elphinstone in his noted Breviary —how the fame of this early Christian martyr spread from the Continent to the north of Scotland, and how a chapel was dedicated to him near the banks of the Dee. It was only as the memory of the saint and his chapel faded that people lost touch with the very meaning of the name Foty, and went from bad to worse in the corrupting course. It hardly needs to be said after these explanations that it was the Chapel of St. Fotin that gave the name to the district of Foty, or Futty, and also to the family name of De Foty, prominent feuars in the neighbourhood, whose best known representative, Laurence de Foty, was twice Provost of Aberdeen in the fifteenth century.*

That interesting name, Foty, is almost the only name in the district that carries us back to a respect-

*The whole subject will be found dealt with in detail by the present writer in an article, "The History and Meaning of 'Footdee'," *Aberdeen Free Press*, 11th August, 1909. This is probably the worst example of a corrupted place-name—certainly it has been one of the most difficult to elucidate—in the district of Aberdeen.

able and enlightening antiquity. There is, indeed, the "Pocra" pier, another corruption, from the "Pow Creek," but there is not even a Block-house Place to indicate where the fort stood for four hundred years till it was cleared away in our own time for the extension of a fish-curing yard.*

After the removal of the fish-town in 1808, and the opening of the shipbuilding yards in that quarter, the whole district of "Footdee" began to fill up. So we find in 1816 a new street laid out there "to be called Wellington Street," after the victor at Waterloo, and at the same date a new street leading towards the quay to be named Church Street, because it is opposite St. Clement's Parish Church—both street names still in use. Close to them is Canal Terrace, which, for the first thirty or forty years of its life, faced the Aberdeenshire Canal. The adjoining Prince Regent Street and York Street are of the same period, and belong to the numerous groups of street names reminiscent of royal personages.

We are now in the region of the harbour where certain of the more notable street names claim attention.

Commerce Street dates from the middle of the eighteenth century, and is an early effect of the Shorelands Improvements and the growing trade of the harbour. In 1760, the new road was made from the

*This is one of the few cases in Aberdeen, however, where a tablet has been placed on the existing building, telling that the Block-house stood there. See Historical Aberdeen, pp. 60 *et seq.*

Quay to Hangman's Brae, near the Castlehill, and it was resolved to pay the cost out of the Bridge of Don charge, "as it leads all goods the nearest way from the Quay to the Old Town and the Bridge of Don."* That was rather a far-fetched excuse for applying the Bridge of Don funds for such a purpose, but it was no one's interest to object, and so it sufficed. On 30th September, 1790, it was decided to carry the street up towards Park Street, as at present, through the ground known as the Bowie Well Croft.

Half-way up its length, Commerce Street is touched by Castle Terrace, already mentioned. The declivity here is still known colloquially as the Hangman's Brae, from the fact that the small, isolated dwelling of the public executioner stood here in the later years of that functionary's existence. The office was abolished by the Magistrates elected under the Burgh Reform Act, 1833, but a street name of that kind which touches the popular imagination is not allowed to die very readily.†

* Council Register, LXII., fol. 278.

† At a meeting of the Reformed Town Council, 27th November, 1833, on the motion of the Dean of Guild, a return was ordered to be made up of all offices or appointments in the gift of the Magistrates, of the persons holding these offices, for what terms, and upon what conditions, and the emoluments of the same. Mr. Emslie, one of the Councillors, observed that there was one office, at least, which they could very well dispense with, he meant the hangman, and if, unfortunately, they ever required his services, such an official could be got from other places at a much cheaper rate than retaining one in Aberdeen when there was no use for him, This led to the abolition of the office. *Aberdeen Journal*, 27th November, 1833. See also as to the foregoing Historical Aberdeen, p. 46.

Adjoining Commerce Street is Sugarhouse Lane. About the middle of the eighteenth century, the new industry of sugar-refining was introduced into Scotland, and the four shipping towns of Glasgow, Greenock, Dundee, and Aberdeen opened a considerable trade with the Southern States of America and the West Indies. It was from this industrial movement that such street names arose as Jamaica Street and Virginia Street in Glasgow, Jamaica Street, Virginia Street, and Sugarhouse Lane in Greenock, Sugarhouse Wynd in Dundee, and Virginia Street and Sugarhouse Lane in Aberdeen. James Moir of Stoneywood, the noted Jacobite (nominated as Governor of Aberdeen for the Jacobites, 1745), was one of the first to begin sugar-refining in Scotland, at his own property of Stoneywood, after his return from exile, but he was not successful. After a short trial it was given up.*

It was in 1776 that a public company, formed chiefly of Aberdeen merchants, took out a feu on the Shorelands belonging to the Town Council, and erected the Sugarhouse in what then became, and still is, Sugarhouse Lane.† I believe part, at least, of the original Sugarhouse is still standing, and it was here that one of the first Industrial Schools of Aberdeen was carried on for some years. The Sugarhouse

* Kennedy's Annals, II., p. 216. For detailed list of notices, etc., relative to this remarkable man, see communication by present writer, *Aberdeen Free Press*, 6th July, 1910.

† May 8, 1776, the Sugarhouse Company of Aberdeen feued a Lot of ground in the Shorelands. Aberdeen Sasine Registers, vol. and page of date.

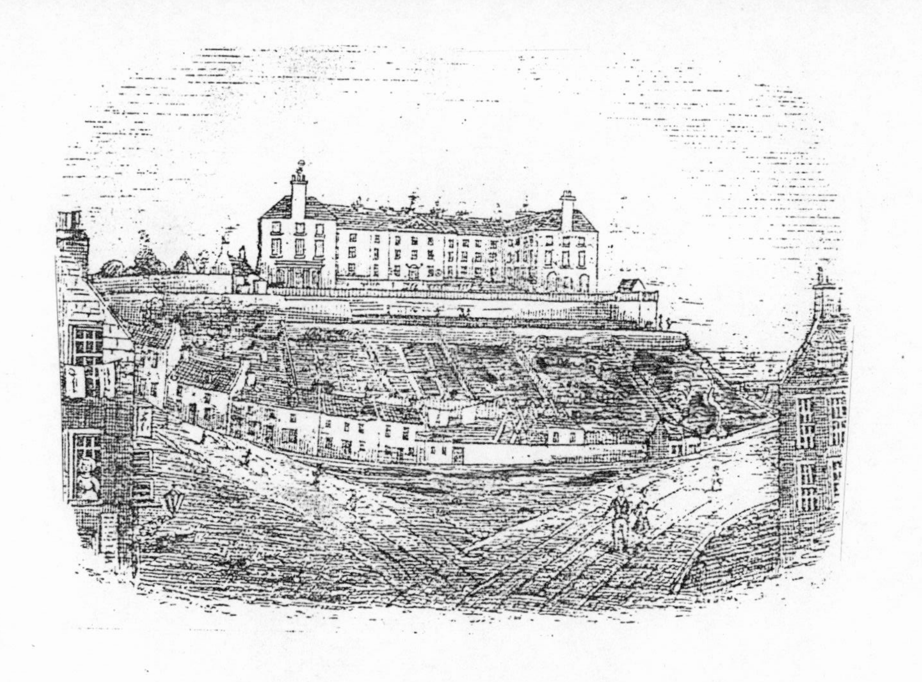

Castlehill, showing Hangman's Brae, *c.* 1830.

Company carried on business for about twenty-five years, but, says Kennedy, who knew personally, "although their capital was abundant, and the credit of the partners undoubted, the undertaking was not attended with that success which they had a right to expect.*

Virginia Street is associated with Sugarhouse Lane, and, as already said, belongs to the same period, and to the same trade development at the harbour.

The explanation of the name Chapel Lane, the adjoining thoroughfare, I owe to the compiler of a most interesting little work, published two years ago—The Book of Melville United Free Church Bazaar. The original members of that congregation were a body of secessionists from the East Church, 1757, whose first place of worship was a tobacco warehouse at the corner of Virginia Street and Weigh-house Square. As the little work above-mentioned says, it was not a promising looking structure. By knocking out windows here and there, and an additional doorway, the secessionists made it passably convenient, and it served as the chapel of this zealous body of Christians until 1772, when they bought the Guild Brethren's Hospital in Correction Wynd, and erected the church building only recently demolished.

Previous to the period of this chapel the lane seems to have had no distinctive name. It was merely a "vennel," and there can be little doubt that it was

*Kennedy's Annals, II., p. 216.

the existence of this primitive chapel building there that led to the name of the Chapel Lane.*

It is singular that Aberdeen has no Trongate (or Tron-gait, to be more accurate, meaning, of course, the road of the Tron), for Aberdeen, as well as Edinburgh, Glasgow, and other towns had its Tron, or Weigh-house, for centuries.

The story of the Weigh-house of Aberdeen, the curious mean-looking structure that was demolished less than thirty years ago, is one of the romances of local history. It recalls that the rights and liberties of Aberdeen—as, indeed, of other towns—rested on its trading privileges. Our earliest charters were charters of trade, granting to the community rights to carry on trade and to levy dues, and giving the promise of peace and protection in carrying on its business.

King Robert the Bruce appears to have granted to Aberdeen the earliest charter entitling the town to exact such dues on merchandise as fell within the Tronarship. The legal institution of the Tron dates, however, from the reign of David II., when the Scots Parliament, sitting at Scone, 6th November, 1347, enacted "that the Chamberlane sall cause big and mak ane Trone for weying of woll in all the kingis burghis, and all the ports of the realme."† The Tron, or Weigh-house as we knew it in Aberdeen, was not establised, however, for many years after that,

*The old chapel building is still standing, and is being used again as a warehouse. A small cut of it is given in the little bazaar book named.

† Sir John Skene's Regiam Majestatem, part II., f. 44.

although troning was duly carried on, and various reforms were effected, particularly in the proper regulation of the weights and measures to be used. Thus, in 1560, the Town Council enacted that no person should keep or use any stone weight to buy or sell by, "except a sufficient stone weight of just ponderation containing 16 trois pound, and ilk trois pound to contain 16 ounces, and all point stoups to be metted and measured and presented to the Baillies."*

At the time of this enactment the Tronarship, or right of exacting dues on merchandise within the burgh, was not in the hands of the community. By a strange and unwarranted interference with the rights of the town, James IV., in 1494, granted to his Admiral, Andrew Wood of Overblairton, the Tron and Tron weights of Aberdeen in perpetuity, and the King did much more than that. He granted to the Admiral also the Castle-hill and the Forest of Stocket—an action that struck at the very roots of the town's existence as an independent burgh, which the townspeople so manfully resented that the grant was annulled by the Privy Council, and the Admiral never really obtained possession.†

In the great struggle that took place between the burgh and the King over the grant of the Castle-hill and Stocket, the Tronarship seems to have been overlooked. In any case, it was enjoyed by Wood and his successors for many years. In 1585, Alexander

*Council Register, XXIV., fol. 10.

†See the episode fully dealt with, Historical Aberdeen, pp. 20-1.

Rutherford purchased the office and its rights, and duly made application to the Magistrates to be infeft with the same, offering to erect a weigh-house, as in Dundee and other towns, "provided the Council will appoint five or six of the Council, with the advice of six or seven of the merchants and traffickers, to consider what sort of gear shall be weighed therein, what shall be paid by him yearly to the town therefor, and what duties shall be taken of all sorts of gear therein weighed, or if the same order and custom shall be observed as in Dundee."*

But the town was now determined to assert its rights. The Magistrates refused to grant the application of Alexander Rutherford, and, in 1590, the question was the subject of a "Head Court" of the inhabitants. That Court, we are told, all in one voice granted and consented to the establishment of a Weigh-house, and made choice of four burgesses of guild to be joined with the Council to consider the articles to be weighed and the dues to be payable.†

That was not quite the end of the dispute, nor the beginning of our Weigh-house, but it foreshadowed both. In 1617, Rutherford yielded the point. He received 1000 merks as compensation, and he granted an acknowledgement of the town's right to the Tronarship as contained in their charter from Robert the Bruce.‡

* Council Register, XXXI., fol. 686.

† Ibid., XXXIII., fol. 1066.

‡ Ibid., XLVIII., ff. 114, 213.

I have no idea as to where the Weigh-house was first situated. Probably it was in different parts of the town, as suited the convenience of the tacksman of the time, as well as of the public. For a long time stone weights were used, and one can well imagine the difficulties that would arise in buying and selling by "stones" of varying weight. It was not till 1560 in Aberdeen that a definite standard was laid down, when, as already explained, a reform in the weights and measures took place. In 1625 stone weights were finally discarded, and iron weights from Flanders took their place.

The old weigh-house and pack-house that stood till a few years ago dated from 1631.* Its timber platform, so familiar a feature in our time, dated from 1707, and was built from the wreck of an Amsterdam vessel which ran ashore on the Belhelvie sands.† Sometimes the Weigh-house was used as a magazine for gunpowder and other warlike stores; in more peaceful times it was used for Town Council election meetings and such like purposes. Merchandise of every kind passed through the Weigh-house, and in the old days, as well as now, owners of such goods were sometimes unmindful of their own. In December, 1841, I find public intimation made of un-

*Kennedy says "about the beginning of the seventeenth century," and Parson Gordon, our first historian, says 1634. The precise date is as above. See Town Council Register, vol. LII., p. 32.

†The story of the wreck, and the appropriation of the ship and cargo by the Aberdonians—uncommonly like an act of brigandage—is told by Kennedy, Annals, vol. II., pp. 261-2.

claimed goods lying at the public Weigh-house, which included a cask of paint, some bundles of steel from London, two bags of nails from Hull, a truss of wine from Rotterdam, a jar of some mysterious substance from Dundee, a bundle of saws from Hull, a basket, a bag of fruit, with other bags and boxes of undetermined contents.

The end of the Weigh-house came with the abolition of the Bell and Petty Customs. Thenceforward, it was used as a potato and grass store on the ground floor, and the upper floor as a sail loft, till 1883, when it was demolished to make way for the new Harbour Offices. These are erected partly on the site of the old structure, and partly in the adjoining open space which had so long and rightly carried the name of Weigh-house Square.

Marischal Street is one of the most interesting of that class of street names which represent former proprietors or feuars of the ground.

Before 1765 there was no direct public access from Castle Street to the Quay between Futty's Wynd on the east, and Shore Brae on the west. The growth of trade at the harbour made a new street absolutely necessary, and suggestions were made that the historic house in Castle Street, which had been the town house of the Earls Marischal for centuries, should be bought by the town, and the new street cut through the site of the house and garden to the Quay. Provost Chalmers, the printer—the same who spent an hour with Burns in the New Inn, on the opposite side of Castle Street, the only house that Burns visited on his way through Aberdeen—was authorised to open up communications with the representatives of the Earl. On September 30, 1765, the Town Council had the result before them:

"30th Sept., 1765.—The said day, the Council, having heard and considered a letter from Lord Marischal in relation to the purchase of his lordship's Lodging in the Castlegate, intended to be made by the town for opening a passage from the Castlegate of this Burgh to the Shore, and erecting a street there, with several letters on the same subject from Mr. Keith, his lordship's Doer [man of business] at Edinburgh to the Provost. They approved of what the Magistrates have already done in this affair, and recommend to and empowered the Magistrates, along with Provost Chalmers, Baillies Robertson and Farquhar, or any five of themselves as a Committee, to conclude a bargain in relation to the said purchase, and to give such adequate price therefor as they shall think reasonable."*

The communications that followed occupied some months, but in April of the following year the transaction was completed, and the Town Council Register bears the record:

"15th April, 1766.—The which day, the Provost reported to the Council that the Magistrates had in consequence of the Council's Act of 30th September last, finished the purchase of Lord Marischal's House and Garden in this place, and had received a Disposition from his Lordship thereto in favour of the Treasurer, who had paid the sum of £803 13*s*. 4*d*. sterling, as the price thereof, including £68 13*s*. 4*d*. as the interest thereof since Whitsunday, 1764. Of all which the Council unanimously Approved, and further recommend to, and Impowered

* Council Register, LXIII., f. 40.

the Magistrates and other Gentlemen of the Council named the 30th of September last, to sett about making out and completing the new street proposed to be carried thorrow Lord Marischal's Lodging and Heritage, and from thence through the Shorelands to the Quay, and to purchase what ground of the Shorelands may be necessary for completing the said street at a reasonable and adequate price."*

It was resolved that the new street should be 40 feet wide, of which 30 feet was laid off as carriage-way, and five feet on each side to be paved for foot passengers. It is stated by some writers that Marischal Street was the first street in Aberdeen to be paved with squared granite setts. That is likely enough to be true.

The bridge, carrying the new street over Virginia Street, was a subject of grave consideration. William Law, architect, who at that time was carrying out certain alterations on the old Greyfriars Church in Broad Street, drew out plans for the new bridge, and a contract was entered into with Alexander Bannerman, mason, to build the bridge according to Law's designs for £590. He did so, although certain "extras" ultimately figured in the account to the amount of £84.† The substantial quality of his work may still be seen, for Bannerman's bridge stands practically as it left his hands nearly a hundred and fifty years ago, and probably will continue to discharge its duties for centuries to come.

*Council Register, LXIII., f. 51.

†Ibid., LXII., ff. 97, 105, 128.

The Weigh House,

c. 1850.

The Earl Marischal's House in the Castlegate, demolished to make way for Marischal Street, was one of the most interesting of the historic houses of Aberdeen. It was there that Mary Queen of Scots lodged on her return journey from the north of Scotland in September and October, 1562, and we are all familiar with the story of how she witnessed (against her will, it is said) from a window of this house the execution of Sir John Gordon, fourth son of the Earl of Huntly, two days after the battle of Corrichie.

Probably no sadder gathering ever took place in Earl Marischal's House than the one only recently made known by the publication of the Calendar of those remarkably interesting Stuart Papers, now preserved at Windsor Castle. It was in September, 1715, after Sheriffmuir, and after the Pretender had secretly slipped away from the broken army, and embarked at Montrose. The noblemen, general officers, and chiefs held a council of war in Earl Marischal's House in Aberdeen, where James's departure was made known to an already disheartened company, and drove them and their followers to the acutest anger and despair.*

The personal associations of Marischal Street are extremely interesting for Aberdonians. One of the earliest residents after the street was formed was Dr. William Dyce, a leading physician of the town, and in his house, still standing, was born in 1806 his son, William Dyce, afterwards R.A., whose really great work in the promotion of British Art is acknowledged

*Calendar of Stuart Papers (Hist. MSS. Commission) vol. II., p. 110.

almost anywhere except in Aberdeen. It would be surely appropriate that the birthplace of Dyce should be distinguished by a modest tablet.* But before William Dyce was able to handle a brush, Marischal Street had already given an eminent artist to the world—Andrew Robertson, celebrated not only as a miniature artist himself, but not unworthy to be named the father of miniature painting in this country.

Then Marischal Street had its literary men too. Until William Kennedy's two quarto volumes, "The Annals of Aberdeen," were given to the world in 1818, the history of the town had never really been told. The house, 46 Marischal Street, stands as it did when William Kennedy, advocate, had his house and office there, where he wrote his "Annals," and where he died in 1836. It was in this same house that John Ramsay, editor of the *Aberdeen Journal*, and a leading spirit of the town for many years, spent his last years, in physical and personal trouble indeed, but always keenly concerned in whatever touched the interests of his native city. One would imagine that this house too might well carry some outward and visible token of its interesting history.

*Dyce's influence in promoting the pre-Raphaelite movement, even in the period of the greatest popular hostility, is only now becoming known through the publication of the Ruskin letters, and the personal memoirs of Millais, Holman Hunt, and others of the innermost group.

CHAPTER V

THE FRENCH ELEMENT IN ABERDEEN STREET NAMES: THE "QUAYS": "PLACE" IN OUR STREET NAMES: THE DERIVATION AND MEANING OF "VENNEL": THE USE OF "ROW": SHIPROW AND ITS STORY: THE STREET NAMES OF THE MARKET QUARTER.

BEING now in the neighbourhood of the harbour, we notice that in Aberdeen, as in other Scottish towns, we have no "wharves." They are all "quays," as in French towns—Waterloo Quay, Regent Quay, Trinity Quay, and so on. This is the French *quai*, meaning a place where vessels are unloaded, and may be set down as a survival of that old Franco-Scottish relationship, to which, perhaps, we are tempted sometimes to ascribe too much, but evidences of which are still far from uncommon in our Scottish place and street names. This use of "quay" is the French usage, continuously retained in Scotland from the middle centuries. We know from the peculiar spelling of the name in many of the official documents of Aberdeen that the derivation of the name seems to have been often lost, a common enough thing in regard to many of our local place names.*

*A curious example of this is the name of the Pow Burn. Pow Burns are common throughout Scotland. Originally, "Pow," a Celtic term denoting a pool or burn, was enough, but

The French influence is seen in other street names in Aberdeen. We have many instances of street names ending in "Place"—Union Place (obsolete), Kingsland Place, Skene Place, Mackie Place, Crimond Place, Rosemount Place, and so on. In this we have a modification of the French term *place*, meaning a wide space or broad way in a town. The uses of the term "Place," however, are extraordinarily varied in this country. In Aberdeen, prior to the Reformation, the word "Place" was used to denote not only a street, but a convent, as well as the whole precincts of a friary, a use that was, of course, quite usual in old Scots Acts of Parliament and other legal documents. In the 15th century a feu charter was granted in the Green of Aberdeen on payment, among other things, of an annual rent of five shillings to the Carmelite Friars and their successors "the friars of the said Place." In 1587 part of the income of the chaplains of St. Nicholas Church came from property in the Shiprow "near the Place of the Holy Trinity," and the same phrase is often used of the property of the Grey Friars in Broad Street. The use of the word to denote a residence, especially a manor house, or residence of that character, has long been common throughout the country, and crops up repeatedly in

as the knowledge of the real meaning was lost, it was thought to be a specific, not a general name, and the word "burn" was added, which meant the same thing. In the same way, one is amused to notice that in Ayr, the fine old street the "Sandgate," leading to the beach, which means, of course, the Sand Road, or the Sand Street, now bears officially the tautological name of Sandgate Street.

literature. It will be remembered that one of Shakespeare's purchases, after he became a person of substance, was the New Place at Stratford; and Scott, in "Guy Mannering," applies the name of Auld Place and New Place to the old and new castles of Ellangowan.*

Another street name which we had from the French was the Vennel, previously Gordon's Wynd, which ran from Gallowgate to the Lochside, and was cleared away in 1842 to make way for St. Paul Street. It is a street name which occurs in nearly all the older Scottish towns, from the old Black Vennel of Inverness and the Little and Muckle Vennels of Cromarty to the Glasgow Vennel of Irvine, where Burns worked as a flax-dresser, and what used to be the Wee Vennel of Dumfries, where also Burns dwelt. Of course, Perth, the ancient capital, has quite a cluster of them. It is the *venelle* of the French, meaning a narrow mean street, used at one time as a general designation of all mean filthy passages. This idea has so possessed the Scottish mind that a "vennel" has become associated throughout Scotland with any place which is so particularly mean and squalid that in the forcible Teutonic it might otherwise be termed a pig-sty.

There is just one other apparently French element in our Aberdeen street names. That is the word "Row," in the names of Shiprow, Guestrow, Union Row, and such like. This has been supposed to represent the familiar term *Rue*, meaning a street in

*I notice that an Aberdeenshire landed proprietor has named his residence the Place of Tillyfour. There are many examples of the use of the term in connection with the manor houses of the same district.

France, and in a small book of mine published some years ago, I ventured to give this as the meaning of the word.* I now think that that is wrong. No doubt the word "rew," spelt "rew," and "rewe," was used in Aberdeen some centuries ago to mean a street in a general sense, and often the town's drummer had instructions from the Town Council to proceed with his intimations through "the haill rewes of the toun." In Greenock, too, we have a street actually bearing the name, Rue-end Street, but I find that that is not a continuous use, but a reversion (and, as I think, a mistaken reversion) to what was supposed to be the original meaning of "Row." There cannot be any doubt, I think, that our word "Row" came to us through the Anglo-Saxon "Raw," sometimes (as in Chaucer) spelt "rewe," which has been used by the Teutonic people as far back as written history goes. And it is in the form of "Raw" that it always appears first in our street names in Aberdeen. Thus we had the Ship-raw, one of our earliest descriptive names, meaning, of course, the road to the harbour; the Exchequer Raw, the Ghaist-raw, and others, all of which it will be our duty to deal with in due time.

The Shiprow is one of the very oldest of our existing streets. Its name under the old Latin form of *Vicus Navium*, Ship Road, occurs as early as the Green, or the Gallowgate, two names expressing social necessities that would arise as early as the burgh itself. The Shiprow was the only road that led from the low ground near the shore to the hill-head on which the

* Historical Aberdeen—chapter on Guestrow.

Castle and the Castlegate came to be situated, so that it has been used as a public highway by countless numbers of persons of all classes through eight centuries that we know of, and probably for centuries before then.*

The incidents connected with this very old street are far more numerous than can be referred to here. At the foot of the Shiprow stood one of the city gates, and through it—for the Shiprow was the main entry from the South up till Union Street was opened in the nineteenth century—more remarkable pageants passed than through all the other five city gates combined. It was in the Shiprow that the heroic Provost, "Sir" Robert Davidson, who marched with the burghers to the battle of Harlaw, had his tavern. He was a notable personage in many ways, a weaver to trade, or at least had the right to use the symbols of the weaver craft, he was a King's official (for he collected the King's customs in Aberdeen), he was the friend of earls, and spokesman in courts of justice for many a citizen of Aberdeen. It is said that it was Provost Davidson who built the Town House in the Castlegate, and although the record of that is, in other respects, obviously a defective document, it may very well be that the credit of making the Castlegate the heart of Aberdeen for all time is due to this enterprising and prosperous citizen.†

*What seems to be the earliest mention of the Shiprow by name, occurs in a charter of annual rents, of date 1281. Registrum Epis. Aberd., II., p. 278.

†The statement that Davidson built the Town House in the Castlegate is contained in the chartulary of St. Nicholas, II., 16.

Certainly, the most curious thing I ever heard with regard to any notable resident in the Shiprow is told of Thomas Spark, for many years clerk and treasurer to the Royal Infirmary. He died in March, 1848, aged 92, and Colonel Johnston of Newton Dee tells that he died in the same house in Shiprow in which he had been born, and out of which he had not slept a single night during his remarkably long life. I should imagine that, in its way, this is one of the strangest cases on record.*

Certain of the Shiprow closes have names that excite interest. There is Abbey Place, with its moulded circular-topped entrance, which at once suggests a monkish house. So far as can be ascertained, however, no abbey ever existed here. A chapel stood on the high ground of St. Katharine's Hill, built by Kennedy, the constable, or Castellan of Aberdeen, in the thirteenth century, and it stood just behind the close now known as Abbey Place, but one can hardly imagine that the name has anything to do with it.†

We are on firmer ground in dealing with the next close, known as Ross's Court, near which stands the

but in a document otherwise marked by errors and clearly written many years after the event.

*The story is told in Colonel Johnston's privately printed but invaluable Memoirs of the Young Family.

†One may note the single old hawthorn tree that still flourishes in the ground within Abbey Place. It has been suggested to me that this is one of the numerous trees that were on St. Katharine's Hill down to the great alterations involved in the making of Union Street. That is, no doubt, quite the case.

Photo by Mr. W. J. Watt.

The Shiprow.

ancient-looking castellated house that attracts the notice of all visitors to the Shiprow. This was the residence of John Ross, of Arnage, Provost of Aberdeen in 1710-1712. The house dates, however, from about the beginning of the 17th century, and with its little forecourt and wall, pierced by the main entrance, has an air of the old French architecture that was not yet so uncommon in certain of the older Scottish towns. It seems to have been built by one Alexander Farquhar, and was afterwards in the possession of James Sinclair of Seba, and James Nicolson of Tarbrown, at one time Dean of Guild of Edinburgh.* Provost Ross of Arnage doubtless made it his town house in the early years of the eighteenth century, and gave his name to the neighbouring Ross's Court.†

Another Shiprow close is Mearns Court. It has nothing to do with Mearns Street in the Shorelands, which is named after Provost Daniel Mearns (still, happily, with us), but was named after a person of the name of Mearns, a stocking manufacturer in Aberdeen, one of the numerous Aberdonians who travelled with his wares in the Low Countries. Mearns's son-in-law was Alexander Robertson, Supervisor of Excise for Aberdeen district, which raises rather an interesting point in local personal history. One of Robertson's officers was Malcolm Gillespie, the noted gauger of Skene, and so friendly was the relationship between

*Mr. Alex. M. Munro, in Old Landmarks of Aberdeen.

†The old house is described and illustrated in MacGibbon and Ross's Castellated and Domestic Architecture of Scotland, v., pp. 78, 80.

the two that Robertson's son (Alexander Robertson, afterwards of Sheffield) often spent his holidays with Gillespie at Crombie Cottage, Skene, where the events took place that resulted in Gillespie's tragic end. It was due to this that a daugher of Gillespie, named Jane Maxwell Gordon after the famous Duchess of Gordon, stayed with Robertson, the supervisor, in Mearns Court, Shiprow, in that dreadful week in November, 1827. After her father's execution, the young lady became a governess in Dr. Dyce's family, Marischal Street, the home of William Dyce, the future R.A.*

The name of Shore Brae needs no explanation, but there is at least one interesting point about the street to be noted. For centuries the Shore Brae was no street at all, in the strict sense; merely an opening in the Shiprow, sloping down to the water's edge—to the "Bulwark" the first portion of the Aberdeen Docks ever built. It seems to have taken its place among the ordinary streets of Aberdeen from about the time of the Jacobite risings, for we find that the Town Council, on July 12, 1746, "Appoint the Treasurer to cause repair the causey (roadway) that leads from the Shiprow to the Shoar, commonly called the Shoar Brae, and to agree with workmen therefore at as easy a charge as possible."†

*The story is told in the papers left by the late Mr. James Rettie, author of Aberdeen Fifty Years Ago. He was personally acquainted with Alexander Robertson, son of the supervisor.

†Council Register, LXI., f. 212.

Market Street, as a name, carries its meaning on its face. The construction of the New Market between 1840 and 1842 brought to a head suggestions that had been made as early as 1825 to lay out a new street there to connect Union Street and the harbour. Archibald Simpson made out plans accordingly for Market Street, and it was constructed by the New Market Company, and made over to the town.* It and the Market buildings obliterated a very old Aberdeen thoroughfare, Putachieside, so named because the proprietor of Castle Forbes, then known as Putachie, had his town house in that street.

Hadden Street belongs, as would be understood, to the same period, and carries the name of that family who not only started Hadden's factory in the Green in the later years of the 18th century, but were eminent in civic affairs in Aberdeen for many years. The Hadden family connection appears in another street name in Aberdeen—Lindsay Street, now an obscure thoroughfare connecting Diamond Street and Golden Square. In 1817, when the Golden Square group of streets were being laid out, Elspet Hadden, daughter of Provost James Hadden of Persley, married Colonel Martin Lindsay, of the 78th Regiment, and I believe it was out of compliment to the Lindsays and the Haddens that this street got its name. It was Charlotte Anne Lindsay, daughter of Colonel Martin

*Simpson's plans for the construction of Market Street are still in existence—the property of Messrs Macandrew and Co., Loch Street. They formed part of a most interesting "Simpson Exhibition" in Aberdeen in November, 1909.

Lindsay and Elspet Hadden who, in 1845, married Alexander Pirie, papermaker, and was the mother of A. C. Pirie, Martin H. Pirie, and the rest of this Stoneywood family, so well known in many parts of the world in connection with their particular industry.

Adelphi, which connects Market Street with Union Street, is said sometimes to have been named from the circumstance that the brothers Pirie, papermakers, at one time had their business offices in the street. That is not so, however. The street was laid out about 1810, although probably only partially constructed then, for in 1815 it is still spoken of as "the new street lately formed in the place called the Adelphi."* It seems to have been sometime after the street was named before the brothers Pirie were connected with it. On 9th January, 1812, Alexander Duncan, quill-maker, got sasine "of the piece of ground lying along the west side of the street lately formed in the place called the Adelphi." † It was on the following 9th February that George and William Pirie were infeft with the same property "in security and relief to them of a Bond of Credit to the Governor and Company of the Bank of Scotland to the extent of £400 sterling."‡ This street name is one

*Register of Sasines, volume of date 24th Aug., 1815.

†Ibid., volume of date.

‡Ibid., volume of date. It is interesting to note, however, that the property of the Piries was a feature of the far end of the Adelphi for about half a century. Their dwelling-house was the last house on the east side of the street; the works were in the old buildings, still standing, between the end of Adelphi

of the cases of the adoption of a London name, from the Adelphi which the brothers Adam had then recently laid out, and it is the relationship of the brothers Adam that the name commemorates. Like the London one, the Aberdeen Adelphi is a *cul de sac.*

The other street names in the Market quarter scarcely call for special explanation. Exchange Street is one of those projected by Archibald Simpson, architect, while he was operating in that quarter for the Market Company, although it was not really opened till after his death. Its name is due to the fact that the Corn Exchange was erected at the top of this street. The ground at the time belonged to the Aberdeen Railway Company—whose station was at first to be erected there, instead of in Guild Street—and in the beginning of 1854 the Company received an offer from persons "who proposed to erect a new Corn Exchange, for a piece of ground forty feet in length along Hadden Street, and seventy feet in length along a new street leading from Hadden Street to Guild Street." The double scheme was carried out in the course of the next few years, and thus Exchange Street came into being.

Carmelite Street and Carmelite Lane are so named as having been laid out in the end of the eighteenth century, partly on the ground of the Carmelite Monastery; and the adjoining Trinity Street, as is well known, was similarly formed on ground once owned by the Trinity

and Shiprow. The workers entered from the Shiprow. In 1862, the works were removed to the then vacant factory buildings at Poynernook.

Friars, whose property was purchased in 1631 by the noted Rev. Dr. Guild, and by him was presented to the Aberdeen Incorporated Trades. It was in this way that the Trades came to be occupants of Trinity Ha', so familiar in local annals, a name still borne by the newer buildings of the Incorporated Trades in Union Street. It was the same Dr. William Guild whose name is perpetuated in the name of Guild Street, for it was there that his benefaction to the Trades was situated when Guild Street, such as it is, was laid out.

I fancy not very many Aberdonians know that in Guild Street there is a "Memorial" of Dr. Guild, whose character as a Covenanting Minister, as Principal of King's College, and public personage generally, has been so much discussed. This is the public fountain known as "Fidler's Well" at the busy corner of Guild Street and Market Street. It was erected in 1857, the two-hundredth anniversary of Dr. Guild's death, by Alexander Fidler, coal merchant at the harbour, and one can see at any hour of the day how useful a purpose the fountain and drinking-trough serve for both man and beast, as the kind-hearted donor intended. The cast-iron fountain has this singular inscription:

FOUNTAINHALL, 1st AUGUST, 1857.

Water springs for man and beast,
At your service I am here;
Although six thousand years of age,
I am caller, clean, and clear.

ERECTED FOR THE INHABITANTS OF THE WORLD
BY
ALEXANDER FIDLER.

This eccentric inscription is worn so smooth as to be nearly unreadable, but anyone can easily make out —although probably few pay heed to—the bold, deep characters cut in the granite drinking-trough near the ground. They tell that the well was

DEDICATED TO
DR. WILLIAM GUILD.
DIED 1657.

LAMMAS. A.F.

This humble memorial, though very useful, has not been much thought of by townsfolk. It had the curious distinction, however, of being reproduced in a London periodical, *The British Workman*, in August, 1859, on which occasion Mr. Fidler's practical benevolence was commended "to the imitation of London philanthropists."*

The street names on the Reclaimed Land on the banks of the Dee are all recent and self-explanatory, with a few exceptions. One of these is Stell Road.

*Dr. Guild's character and public actions have been much discussed, but perhaps sufficient allowance has not been made for the tragic relationships of his own family circle. He was the second William of the family. The first William, his elder brother, was slain, in 1584, by one John Lesly, who would doubtless be executed for the murder. (Sum Notabill Thinges, p. 20). This was a few years after the Guilds' serving-man had been accidentally drowned at the beach, while bathing. (Ibid., p. 16). Then in 1604 (William Guild being then a young man of eighteen), his brother Robert was found guilty of murdering one Alex. Blair, and sentenced—"his heid to be taken off, and his richt hand, quhilk committed the said slaughter, and big knife put thairin and set on the Tolbuith in example to others in tym to cum." (Surname of Shand, p. 17).

It is interesting to find such a name there. In many of our older towns in England and Scotland, situated near salmon rivers, there were Stell fishings, meaning by that, special pools where net salmon fishing was carried on. Stell Road in Aberdeen takes its name from the adjoining Stell fishings on the Dee, well known for centuries to all concerned in such things.*

Raik Road and Old Ford Road are associated with Stell Road, and it was on the recommendation of the Harbour Board, proprietors of the fishings, that these names were sanctioned by the Town Council as the designations of the new streets, 15th June, 1891. The Raik was an old and well known fishing on the Dee. In 1491, the Town Council and Community of Aberdeen were adjudged by the Lord Auditors to pay to Mr. Andrew Caidzow a half-net of the Raik fishings, with other compensation, for fish which they had wrongfully withheld from him.†

Poynernook Road is another street name in this quarter that might puzzle anyone not acquainted with old burgh history and customs. It comes from the "pynours," or Shore Porters—the "pioniers" of old Scots Acts of Parliament—a well known and useful class of men in Aberdeen for the last four hundred years. They must have had their head-quarters at one time at what has been known as Poyner Nook for the last century and a half at least.‡

*The Stell salmon fishings on the Ness were recently let by the Inverness Town Council at a rental of £120.

†Acts of the Lords Auditors, 19th May, 1491.

‡Their story has been admirably told in the *brochure*, the Aberdeen Pynours, by Mr. John Bulloch.

The Narrow Wynd,

c. 1788

CHAPTER VI

THE EXCHEQUER ROW AND THE MINT: UNION STREET: ROTTEN ROW: THE NARROW WYND: NETHERKIRKGATE AND THE WALLACE NOOK: CARNEGIE'S BRAE: JOHN PHILLIP, R.A.: THE GUESTROW: SOME BROADGATE LANES AND COURTS: CRUDEN AND THE "CONCORDANCE."

WE retrace our steps from the neighbourhood of the harbour, by way of Shiprow, to that ancient little street which connects Shiprow with the Castlegate, namely, Exchequer Row. It is sufficiently well known as one of the narrow "slum" alleys of Aberdeen, but when, prior to the making of Union Street a century ago, it was a main route to the heart of the city, it was narrower still. In 1791 the Town Council took steps to widen Exchequer Row, and what it must have been before then—and remember it was the street along which many a kingly and queenly progress was made in the old days—it is difficult to imagine. We note, as a curious fact, that at the date of that "improvement," William Carnegie, the Town Clerk, had a house in Exchequer Row (although he had also the property of Cornhill House), and for more than a quarter of a century after that time.

The name of Exchequer Row is as interesting as any that we have. We are usually told—I find that some years ago I said so myself in a small work of mine—

that it took its name from the fact that the Aberdeen Mint was situated here, or that it was because the Exchequer and the Mint were here. In point of fact, the Mint had nothing really to do with the name, and the proof of that is rather interesting.

In the early days this street was sometimes spoken of by the very strange name of Skakkarium. Thus, in 1457, a chapel was endowed in St. Machar Cathedral, and part of the endowment consisted of the rent of lands (or houses) of Richard Vaus "lying in the Castlegate of Aberdeen, in the place commonly called Scakkarium."* We get the secret of the name in the Exchequer Rolls of Scotland when, under date 1358, we are told of the rent of the Skakkarium, or King's Custom House in Aberdeen, amounting to six shillings and eightpence. Now, the Custom House, where the accounts of the customs-gatherers were audited, was named in England the Exchequer, or Scaccarium, from a very early date, from the chequered cloth that covered the table.† Soon afterwards the practice spread to Scotland, and evidently the very earliest name of this little street was the "Skakkarium," which in due time gave place to the more understandable name of Exchequer Raw.‡

But there is no doubt that the Mint, although, strictly speaking, it had nothing to do with the name

*Registrum Epis. Aberdonensis, I., p. 281.

†Exchequer Rolls of Scotland. I., Pref. xxxiii.

‡It may be known that to this day the official title of the Exchequer Rolls of Scotland is "Rotuli Scaccarii Regum Scotorum."

of the street, was also situated in Exchequer Row, and for centuries the money of Aberdeen was coined there. It seems impossible to get at the precise date of either the founding of the Aberdeen Mint, or its discontinuance. Kennedy, in his "Annals," says it was founded by William the Lion, about 1211, but no Aberdeen coin of such an early date has ever been recorded. No doubt we are coming very near it. In the Museum of Antiquities, Edinburgh, there are five sterlings of the Aberdeen Mint, of Alexander III., (1249-1283), a number of groats and half-groats of David II. (1329-1370), and quite a parcel of groats of Robert III., (1390-1406); and in the very interesting collection of coins preserved in Gordon's College, Aberdeen, there is also a groat piece of David II., so that it may very well be that Kennedy is right. In any case, the Aberdeen Mint continued to issue coins of one kind or another down to the time of James IV., at least, and the city has had few more interesting institutions. The Mint is supposed to have stood between Stronach's Close and Burnett's Close, and a fine coat of arms, said to have been in the old building that was looked upon as the Mint, now adorns the front of the Chairman's desk in the Mitchell Hall, Marischal College.*

We now reach Union Street, and the meaning of that street name is so well understood that it is only

*It is worth noting that when the Duke of Cumberland was in Aberdeen, 1746, on his way to Culloden, copper money was minted for the use of the Royalist forces in the Quakers' Meeting House, in Guestrow. A roll of the sheet copper used in the process was found in the building after the departure of the troops.

necessary to mention it in passing. The Act of Parliament which authorised the great undertaking of forming two new main avenues in Aberdeen—one from the Castlegate, striking northwards, afterwards named King Street, in honour of the reigning monarch, and the other from the Castlegate westward, cutting through St. Katharine's Hill and bridging the valley of the Denburn—became law on April, 4, 1800. In that same year, viz., on July 2, 1800, the Union of Great Britain and Ireland was accomplished, and the name Union Street was given to the new thoroughfare to commemorate that happy event. The same thing was done in other towns, and Union Streets are not uncommon, dating from the same period.*

Before Union Street was formed (and for some years afterwards) if, instead of turning into Exchequer Row, you held on up Shiprow, you would have entered a narrow little street bearing the name of Rotten Row. It was practically a continuation of Shiprow, across the Netherkirkgate, into Guestrow. It was a very old street, going back in local annals to, at least, the middle of the fifteenth century, and was spelt variously Rotten Row, Rattoun Raw, and Rattenraw. What the meaning of the name was nobody can tell, but, like the Vennels, it was very common in Scottish towns. They have nearly all dropped off now, leaving only one Rotten Row, surely

*Fuller details of the movement for the making of Union Street will be found in The Green and its Story, pp. 26, *et seq.*

the aristocrat of the family, famous all the world over as the fashionable drive in Hyde Park.*

The site of Rotten Row is pretty nearly occupied now by Union Lane. Next to it is St. Katharine's Wynd, interesting as retaining the name of St. Katharine's Hill, the eminence through which Union Street was cut at this part. The name arose from the little chapel that was built on the hill in the thirteenth century, which was dedicated to St. Katharine.

The well known Narrow Wynd ran east and west from the Castlegate to the top of the Shiprow, near Rotten Row, for centuries. Union Street was formed partly on the site of it which occasioned the removal of the buildings along the south side of the Narrow Wynd, and their place is now occupied by Union Buildings, the block designed by Archibald Simpson in 1820. The most notable establishment in the Narrow Wynd was the shop of Alexander Angus & Son, booksellers, the public lounge and political exchange of Aberdeen for years. The houses of the north side of the Narrow Wynd remained till 1867 when they were demolished to make way for the new Municipal Buildings. About the same time the Narrow Wynd Society, the most noted of the old friendly societies of the town, instituted in 1660, ceased to exist.†

*Among the many suggested meanings of the name Rotten Row, perhaps the most fantastic is Route de Roi, Road of the King. That might do for Hyde Park, but not for Aberdeen, or Forfar, or Arbroath, or for the east end of Glasgow.

†The Narrow Wynd Society was quite a well-to-do body. It owned at one time the old Mill of Maidencraig. On occasion it entertained the Povost to dinner.

We are now at Netherkirkgate, and the name need occupy but a moment. One of the city gates stood here—but again, as in the case of the Gallowgate and other streets, the name has nothing to do with that kind of gate. It is "gait," meaning a road or way, and so Nether Kirkgate means the Nether or Lower Kirk-road, just as Upperkirkgate means the Upper Kirk-road. We may be thankful that these interesting old descriptive names have never been changed, and that they are still left to remind us of the paths taken by our forefathers to the old St. Nicholas Church as far back as the twelfth or thirteenth century.

By far the most interesting existing property in Netherkirkgate is the picturesque old building known as the Wallace Tower, or the Wallace Nook. It need hardly be said that the national hero never had anything to do with the building. At one time it was known as Benholm's Tower, and there is some reason to believe that it was at one time the property of Keith of Benholm, a near kinsman of George, fifth Earl Marischal, founder of Marischal College.* The origin of the Wallace legend is to be found probably in the sturdy figure of a soldier, with a sword, which occupies a niche in the tower. This figure—which may have been a recumbent figure from the adjoining St. Nicholas Churchyard—is said to have been put up about the middle of the eighteenth century by one

*It was still sometimes spoken of as Benholm's Neuk in the end of the 18th century. See Fittler's Scotia Depicta published at that time. The coat of arms, supported by the two harts, proper, of the Keiths, may still be seen on the Tower.

John Niven, a tobacco and snuff manufacturer, whose son, Henry, was knighted by George IV. He was the bearer of an address when the Princess Charlotte was married to Prince Leopold.* A story is sometimes seen in print that the name is really the Well House Tower, and arose from the fact that one of the old street wells stood near it, outside the Netherkirkgate port. That story is due to a mere suggestion by Joseph Robertson in the "Aberdeen Magazine," of 1832, that as such was found to be the real meaning of the "Wallace" Tower in Edinburgh Castle, it might be the same with the Wallace Tower in Aberdeen. It is clearly not so, and we must just continue to work with the Wallace tradition, amused a little at the quaint and unwarlike figure which has presented itself to passing generations of Aberdonians as an embodiment of the Champion of Scotland.†

Two minor streets which run off the Netherkirkgate have personal names, one of which, at least, has been more or less a puzzle up till now. This is Carnegie's Brae, still paved with the old cobble-stones of historic times, which slopes down by the back of the Town and County Bank building to the bridge, and so

*From MSS. left by the late Mr. James Rettie, author of Aberdeen Fifty Years Ago.

†Joseph Robertson's article in the "Aberdeen Magazine" of 1832, was accompanied by a fine drawing of the building by James Skene of Rubislaw, the friend of Walter Scott. It is unfortunate, for the satisfactory discussion of the history of this property, that existing title deeds and writs relating to it go back only as far as 1768.

under Union Street. Here we see all that remains of the old Putachieside, partly destroyed by the making of Union Street, and finally cleared away by the construction of the New Market and Market Street in 1840-42. The Carnegie whose name occurs in the street name was James Carnegie, litster (*i.e.* dyer), father of Alexander Carnegie, Town Clerk. The litster died in the middle of the eighteenth century. His connection with Carnegie's Brae is shown by the following public intimation of 1752:

> "Carnegie's Brae—That Tenement of Inland, with the Close, Yard, and Pertinents belonging to the heirs of the deceased James Carnegie, Litster in Aberdeen, lying on the south side of the Netherkirkgate of Aberdeen, without the Port, is to be set in tack to the highest bidder for three or more years after Whitsunday next, ... as also a little House in Putachieside, adjacent to the said Tenement of Inland is to be set in tack, time, and place aforesaid."*

James Carnegie, the litster, had married a daughter of Alexander Thomson, who was Town Clerk of Aberdeen from 1694 to 1724. His own son, Alexander Carnegie, became Town Clerk in 1762, remaining in office till 1793, when he was succeeded by his son, William Carnegie, who was Town Clerk till his death in 1840. He was followed by John Angus, the well known Town Clerk of a more recent generation.†

***Aberdeen Journal*, 10th October, 1752.

†An interesting collection of portraits of Town Clerks in Aberdeen has been brought together in recent years in the Town House by Dr. Gordon, the present Town Clerk. The portraits begin with Alexander Thomson, above mentioned.

From an old print

The Wallace Tower.

Showing Netherkirkgate and Carnegie's Brae, *c.* 1850.

Carnegie's Brae has associations with one of Aberdeen's most famous artists which must not be forgotten. The cellar still in existence there, behind the Wallace Tower, was the workshop of Robert Spark, painter and glazier, where John Phillip, the future R.A., served his apprenticeship as a house-painter. It was then "No. 4 Wallace Nook, Carnegie's Brae."

The other minor thoroughfare in this quarter is M'Combie's Court, which connects Netherkirkgate with Union Street, Thomas M'Combie was a Baillie in Aberdeen in the opening years of last century, who not only gave his name to this passage, but, with others of his family, he made famous a particular brand of snuff. Baillie M'Combie built a new house in Netherkirkgate in 1814, and the Court was formed then. It was recommended then that "it should be paved with flat stones in the manner of the entry of Rotten Row to Union Street."*

We now reach the Guestrow, a street name which has excited more speculation as to its meaning, I suppose, than any other street name in Aberdeen. It is the only Guestrow in existence, so the cause that gave rise to it must be strictly local; and as it is as old as the earlier part of the fifteenth century at least, when streets were known by strictly descriptive designations, the name must have a perfectly natural and easily understood meaning.

The origin of the name we find in the nearness of the street to St. Nicholas Churchyard. In the old

*Police Commissioners' Minutes, II., 164.

days no houses intervened between this street and the churchyard, and so the residents, it was supposed, would see the ghosts of the churchyard in their nightly walks, and hence they came to speak of the street as the Ghaist-Raw. That this was actually the meaning of the name is placed beyond a doubt by the fact that in the old Latin charters it is designated Vicus Lemurum, Road of the Spirits, which is as near as they could come to the understood meaning of the Ghaist Raw.*

At length we emerge on the Broadgate, a name we now know familiarly to mean the Broad-gait, that is the Broad-road, or "Broad-way," as they have it in America. I am rather doubtful if the name Broadgate—or, Braidgate, as it used to be—was ever applied in the early days in the same independent sense as, for example, Castlegate, or Upper Kirkgate. At one time it was spoken of as the Braidgate of the Gallowgate, and in the fifteenth century we find it spoken of as the New Raw of the Gallowgate.† On the whole, therefore, it seems likely that for a long time it was looked upon as part of the Gallowgate, until the inevitable shortening process set in, and we got the "Braidgate" as a separate name.

*I have dealt with the name very briefly here, having already discussed it fully in Historical Aberdeen, pp. 153-159.

†About 1454 John Livingtone, Vicar of Inverugie, founded a chapel in St. Nicholas Church, and part of the endowment was an annual rent of six shillings from John Stevenson's "land" lying in "the Newraw of the Gallowgate." Chartulary of St. Nicholas, I., p. 263.

It used to be supposed that this street was named the Broadgate because no line of houses intervened between it and the Guestrow, that, in point of fact, it included the Guestrow. This is quite an error. Guestrow is one of the early independent streets of the burgh, probably quite as early as the Gallowgate itself.*

Connected with the Broadgate, one or two subsidiary street names are well worthy of notice.

First of all comes the Huxter Row, cleared away on the erection of the present Municipal Buildings forty years ago. A huxter—or better still, huckster—as is well enough known, is just a dealer in small articles.† And so the Huckster Row took its name, naturally enough from the small booths, or shops, that lined the little street for many years. Indeed, its other name was the Booth Row, and we find in 1440 that part of the revenues of the Altar of the Virgin in St. Nicholas was six and eightpence "from the land (or house) of Thomas Blyndsell lying in the Buthrawe" of the Gallowgate; and in 1440 rents were drawn "from the bothie (booths) of Stephen, the son of John, in the Gallowgate and the Buthraw."‡

Next to the Huxter Row was Concert Court, so named from the weekly concerts held there for many years by the once celebrated Aberdeen Musical

*This point is discussed in detail in Historical Aberdeen, pp. 159, *et seq.*

†Same as hawker, to carry one's goods on one's back.

‡Chartulary of St. Nicholas, I., pp. 60, etc.

Society. Concert Court partly remains, the small street behind the Town House, leading from Broad Street to the Advocates' Hall, and its story is closely associated with the later history of the city at various points. The little Episcopal Chapel in Concert Court was one of the places in Aberdeen that were shamefully used by the soldiers of Cumberland in 1746. It was rather a new era for the Court when the Aberdeen advocates, forsaking the fine building built for them by John Smith, City Architect, in 1838 at the corner of the Back Wynd—afterwards known as the Queen's Rooms—erected there the present spacious house for their meetings and for their library. The old associations were finally broken when, in 1869, the whole properties from Concert Court to Union Street began to be demolished to make way for the new Municipal Buildings.

Cruden's Court, in Broad Street, recalls the eccentric but worthy and public-spirited compiler of the "Concordance to the Holy Scriptures." The Court had its name from Baillie William Cruden, father of Alexander Cruden, of the above well-known work. Here, no doubt, Alexander Cruden passed his boyhood and youth, as a student at Marischal College, prior to his departure for London. It was probably here too, that he was residing near the close of his life—"now living in Aberdeen," he says—when he drew up the document by which he bequeathed £100 of stock in the Stationers' Company of London to found a bursary in Marischal College, as also his share in the profits of the "Concordance" to the Town

Council in order that they might present to "seriously disposed persons" copies of certain specified religious works, whose titles alone recall the heroic age of theological discussion in Scotland.

CHAPTER VII

QUEEN STREET AND ITS ASSOCIATIONS: THE "ABERDEEN HERALD": LODGE WALK: THE "CHRONICLE" AND CHRONICLE LANE: LONG ACRE: BAILLIE RAGG AND RAGG'S LANE: THE UPPERKIRKGATE PORT: LITTLEJOHN STREET AND THE GALLOWGATE QUARTER: REMOVAL OF THE GALLOWGATE PORT.

THE name of Queen Street presents no great difficulty. The only question is—which Queen? As the formation of the street was resolved upon in 1773, it was obviously the Queen of George III., but the story of its formation is worthy of a brief notice.

It began in 1764, when a petition was presented to the Town Council, setting forth the inconvenience many people felt in getting at the Flesh Market (then situated near where the North Parish Church now stands), and calling on the Council to lay out a new thoroughfare from the Broadgate to the Back Cause way, that is, the North Street. The Council were sympathetic, but nothing was done for nearly ten years. It was not yet the period of the zealous Police Commissioners. In 1773, the matter again came before the ruling authority:—

"30th Nov., 1773—The said day, there was laid before the Council a petition and representation of date the 20th Nov. last, signed by upwards of sixty of the principal burghers and inhabitants, setting forth the great inconvenience which the inhabitants of the Broadgate and Guestrow and all the west part of the town suffered by having no access to the Flesh and Meal Markets, but either by the Castlegate or East Street, which was a considerable way about; and for obviating these inconveniences the petitioners earnestly recommend to the Council to purchase the house and yard in the middle of the Broadgate, belonging to Andrew Thomson of Crawton, which was presently in the market, and to lay out a new street through the same, and the ground behind it from the Broadgate to the north end of the Lodge Walk, which the petitioners thought would be highly conducive not only to the regularity and ornamenting of that particular part, but to the public good of the town. Which, being heard and considered by the Council, they appoint the same, as being a matter of importance, to lie on the table, and to be continued till next Council day, so as the whole members of the Council may have time deliberately to consider thereof." *

The project so caught the fancy of the Town Council that at the next meeting the laying out of the new street was agreed upon, and within a few months the house of Andrew Thomson, advocate, was duly bought at the price of £620. We are now within the period when the Town Council had begun to name the streets in a formal way, and so this enactment, of date, 25th October, 1775, is of special significance:—

"The said day, the [Town] Council resolve that the new street lately made out from the Broadgate to the Back Causeway and Public Markets shall be called Queen Street in time coming." †

*Council Register, vol. LXIV., f. 6.

†Ibid., vol. LXIV., f. 90.

It was almost immediately after the formation of Queen Street that John Wesley, who had visited Aberdeen for the first time in 1761, built the first Methodist Chapel opened in the town. The Chapel stood on the north side of the street, a hexagonal structure, and was repeatedly used by Wesley himself when he visited the north of Scotland.* Adjoining Wesley's Chapel was built, in 1780, one of the earliest theatres possessed by Aberdeen. "Mad Sinclair," the eccentric schoolmaster, had his chair in the gallery, and round it gathered those who, at his bidding, made or marred a play, after the manner of the *claque* in larger theatrical spheres. Lord Byron, on being brought as a child to Aberdeen, lived first in Queen Street before removal to 64 Broad Street, in the house No. 10 Queen Street, still standing, opposite Greyfriars Church. The Broad Street Byron House has now been cleared away for the extended University Buildings.

Queen Street has its literary associations otherwise—few of the older streets of the town lack them. One of its most notable local poets was John Mitchell, author of "Radical Rhymes," the acknowledged leader of a section of the Aberdeen Chartists about 1840. He opened a bookseller's shop in Queen Street, and subsequently became editor and proprietor of the short-lived *Aberdeen Review*.† From the familiar

*It was used for some time by Rev. Hugh Hart, the eccentric pastor of Zion Chapel, Shiprow, after the closing of that edifice on the formation of Market Street, 1840.

†For the best sketch of Mitchell see Mr. William Walker's Bards of Bon-Accord, pp. 459-62.

Queen Street.

Showing entrance to house where Byron lived.

building at the top of Queen Street—also cleared away for the University extensions—the *Aberdeen Herald* was published down till its incorporation with the *Weekly Free Press* in 1876. It is not too much to say that the *Herald* was the centre of the literary interest of Aberdeen and the north of Scotland throughout a large part of its career. It was through its means that William Thom first found his feet and became known to the world. Its sub-editor for a few years, William Forsyth, gave us some of the most exquisite lyrical pieces which the north country has produced, and he expressed his fondness for Aberdeen in terms so graceful and sincere as to endear it and him to all who take pride in this "Silver City," which he loved so well—

> "I'll love thee till my tongue be mute,
> For all thy fame of ancient years,
> Thy tender heart and resolute,
> Thy tale of glory and of tears;
> The might that from thy bosom springs,
> To fire thy sons where'er they be,
> And for a thousand noble things—
> Brave City by the Sea!
> Bonaillie, O Bonaillie!
> My Silver City by the Sea!" *

The property that was for so many years the *Herald* Office was a building of considerable architectural character—one of the best in the street often spoken of in the old days as the "genteel" Queen Street. Its wide ornamental doorway led into a

*From Idylls and Lyrics, 1872.

spacious passage, whence a fine stone staircase led to the first and second floors, the rooms of which had carved timber and marble mantelpieces. In the basement, near the door of the wine celler, was the deep draw-well that was often a needful adjunct of the better class houses in the town. Before it was occupied as the *Herald* Office, the house was the residence of the Commissioner of the Premier Earl of Aberdeen, the grandfather of the present Earl.

The names of two minor streets in that quarter must often have puzzled many people. One is Lodge Walk, which runs between Queen Street and Castle Street. In 1754, the Aberdeen Lodge of Free Masons acquired a house and garden in the Castlegate for the building of new Lodge premises. Here they erected the well known tavern known as the New Inn, which was the principal hotel (as we should now say) not only in Aberdeen, but north of Edinburgh for more than half a century. The Mason Hall was in the upper story of the New Inn, and entrance was obtained to it from under the archway which connected the New Inn and the Tolbooth. To facilitate entrance to their premises, at the same time as a matter of public convenience, the Free Masons laid out the narrow street behind their property, which from this cause became known as the Lodge Walk. In this street ground was given off by Sheriff Moir of Scotstown, in 1817, for a new Court House and Jail, hence the police establishment came to be situated there. In Lodge Walk, too, an actual historian of Aberdeen dwelt, for Alexander Ross, mender of china, Lodge Walk, sometimes known as "Statio" Ross, issued the "Antiquities of Aberdeen" in thirteen parts, at a penny a number, "or the whole for one shilling, together with a poetical address."*

The New Inn property was bought in 1839 by the North of Scotland Banking Company, and in the fine corner site was erected the bank building which is so conspicuous and familiar a feature still in that neighbourhood.†

The other puzzling street name in this quarter is Shoe Lane—opposite Lodge Walk in Queen Street. It take its name from the fact that, soon after the making of Queen Street, it was laid out by the shoemaker craft of the Incorporated Trades. On 31st January, 1785, the Town Council, on a petition by the shoemaker trade, agreed to place two lamps "in the street or lane called Shoe Lane," but they stipulated "that the said lane shall be used and employed as a public street in all time coming."

In this same neighbourhood is Chronicle Lane, originally Chronicle Street. It took its name from the circumstance that the periodical, *The Aberdeen*

*A very amusing sketch of "Statio" Ross will be found in the late Dr. Alexander Walker's Aberdeen Characters, leaflet, No. 3.

†When the Banking Company stepped in and secured this fine site, arrangements were in progress for building there a large new hotel, to take the place of the New Inn. Isaac Machray, of the Royal Hotel, was having plans of the new hotel drawn, some of which are still in existence. The last of the stock and furnishings of the New Inn were sold by auction on 3rd May, 1839.

Chronicle, was printed there by John Booth in the early years of last century. The *Chronicle* was started by Dr. George Kerr, a physician of ideas—sometimes curious ideas, for he published a work to disprove the circulation of the blood. It had a varied career of a quarter of a century till Saturday 25th August, 1832, when it quietly passed away. It was succeeded by the *Aberdeen Herald*, already spoken of, which came out for the first time on the following Saturday, 1st September, 1832.

In this same quarter was the strangely named Luxembourg Close. It began near the New Inn, King Street, and turned down to West North Street, running between Lodge Walk and King Street, adjoining what used to be the Poultry Market. How it came by its designation it is most difficult to say—just as it seems impossible to get at the origin of the similarly named Patagonian Close, at Belmont Street, belonging to the same period. It is due to the freedom with which, in those days, feuars were allowed to lay out semi-private thoroughfares, and apply to them any name that struck their fancy.

By the extension of Marischal College the long-familiar Long Acre has been very nearly obliterated. It never was much of a street, a circumstance that often happened in the old days when feuars were at liberty to lay out streets on their own ground of any dimensions they considered right and gave most prospect of a quick return for their outlay.

Long Acre, first known as Long Acre Street, was so named after the London street of that name, a practice followed in the case of Spring Gardens, Adelphi, Mile End, Whitehall, and others that we have mentioned. In May, 1783, Arthur Dingwall Fordyce, advocate, who owned property at this part, offered to give off to the town a portion of his ground adjacent to Greyfriars Church for the purpose of making an access to that church more easy and commodious than was then in use. A committee of the Town Council, who visited the ground, came to the opinion "that the additional passage proposed by Mr. Fordyce is altogether unnecessary," and so the matter dropped so far as the public authorities were concerned. But Mr. Dingwall Fordyce went on with his "passage," and in December of 1784 Long Acre Street was in full existence, for we find a petition being presented to the Town Council "craving that the Council would ordain some public lamps to be put in that street, along with the other streets in town—with a declaration thereto subjoined by Mr. Dingwall Fordyce of Culsh, the original proprietor and feuar of the stances of the said street agreeing that the same be declared a public street." All which was done accordingly.

From its earliest years, Long Acre seems to have attracted printers, and from its printing presses issued pamphlets and periodicals for many years—most of which are properly enough forgotten except by bibliographers. A sample of their quality will be found in the "Aberdeen Pirate," of the early part of last century, with a number of the same kind in the "Aberdeen Mirror," the "Aberdeen Shaver" and "Young Shaver," the "Aberdeen Gleaner," the

"Letter of Marque," the "Monitor," and the rest. The sort of literature represented in certain of these last century periodicals would not now be tolerated for a month, and it makes one thankful, all things considered, for the serious mindedness, and dignity, and truthfulness of the press of our own day.

On the opposite side of Broad Street from Queen Street and Long Acre are two short streets connecting with Guestrow, of a more respectable antiquity than either of those just named. They are Blairton Lane and Ragg's Lane. These street names are at least two hundred years old. The former has been variously Blairton's Wynd, Blairton's Lane, and Blairton Lane, and I believe, takes its name from the Laird of Blairton, in Belhelvie, who had property in town, but the actual connection between him and the lane I have not yet discovered.* Ragg's Lane—known also at one time as Baillie Ragg's Wynd—takes its name from Alexander Ragg, a prosperous merchant of the neighbourhood, who was one of the Magistrates of the town continuously from 1694 to 1701 with the exception of one year, 1697. On the 17th July, 1680, he and Margaret Pyper were married;† and on 15th April, 1702, Baillie Alexander Ragg, and his son, William, were granted sasine of the tenement of inland that formerly belonged to Robert Cruickshank in the

*On 24th July, 1723, Isobel Toash, relict of Blairton, was buried near the West Dyke of St. Nicholas Churchyard. (St. Nicholas Burial Register). This is doubtless the same family.

†St. Nicholas Marriage Register. (Extract by Rev. James Smith, St. George's-in-the-West)

Ghaist-Raw of Aberdeen.* Baillie Ragg died in 1719. His tombstone lay at one time in the middle of the front Churchyard of St. Nicholas, but is now in the path in front of the West Church door. There generations of footsteps have quite obliterated its inscription, which, but for the care and forethought of a single individual, would now be wholly lost.†

The Upperkirkgate need not detain us long. One of the city gates was here, but as in the case of the Gallowgate, the name of the street has nothing to do with it. It is the Upper Kirk-gait, or Road, as distinguished from the Nether (or Lower) Kirk-gait, these being the two roads that led from the town on the east to St. Nicholas Church on the west. The Upperkirkgate port, or gateway, was the last of the city gates to be pulled down. It was standing till as late as 1794. Previously, the Town Council bargained in the matter of the port as follows:

> "25th May, 1793—The said day, Baillie Ritchie acquainted the Council that James Black, merchant in Aberdeen, had been communing with him concerning the disposal and sale to the Treasurer for behoof of the community of part of his Tenement of Foreland on the north side of the Upperkirkgate, consisting of the room or chamber above the Upperkirkgate Port and two brick toofalls adjoining, lying immediately upon the north side

*Register of Sasines, vol. 1700 to 1709.

†The inscription is preserved by Mr. Gibb in his extremely valuable "Sketches of Monuments and inscribed Slabs in the Churchyard of St. Nicholas, Aberdeen," of which the single copy in existence is in the Aberdeen Public Library.

of the High Street, and that it was probable Mr. Black would be prevailed upon to make such a sale upon reasonable and moderate terms. Which having been considered by the Council, they authorise and empower Baillie Ritchie to conclude the bargain with the said James Black for the purchase of the said Chamber and toofalls in name of the Treasurer of Aberdeen at any price not exceeding One Hundred and Seventy Pounds Sterling, payable when the whole of the materials thereof are taken down and removed. And which materials are to belong to the said James Black, and to be disposed of as he shall incline."*

The work of demolishing the port must have been set about at once, for the *Aberdeen Journal* of 30th June, 1794, tells us that "The workmen have now finished pulling down the Upperkirkgate Port."† This chamber over the Upperkirkgate Port is the room said to have been occupied by Samuel Rutherford on his banishment to Aberdeen, 1636-1638, from which he wrote the marvellous series of letters that have been of such influence in the religious life of the country.‡ Not far from the same spot, in a house still standing in Crown Court, Upperkirkgate, James Beattie, of the "The Minstrel," lived and died. He and Rutherford were men of very different types, but both had genius, and it is something to have the

*Council Register, LXVI., fol. 246.

†This interesting note from the *Journal* of 1794 I owe to Mr. Donald Sinclair, solicitor.

‡See this whole matter dealt with in the chapter, "Samuel Rutherford in Aberdeen," in the volume, The Lone Shieling, pp. 127-134.

Upperkirkgate.

Showing entrance to Drum's Lane.

associations of both in the compass of one short, narrow street.*

We pass now into the Gallowgate, and alongside the Marischal College buildings we find Littlejohn Street, which is specially interesting as being one of the very first streets in Aberdeen to be named in a formal way.

The projector of this street was William Littlejohn, wright and architect (great-grandfather of Dr. David Littlejohn, Sheriff Clerk). He owned several tenements and yards on the east side of Gallowgate, adjoining the proposed new street. In 1759, the Town Council, at William Littlejohn's request, fixed the boundries of his new house, which he thereafter erected at the top of the new street, and the street itself was completed in 1764. Then we have this official entry of the name—along with that of another new street—and so far as I have been able to discover, it is the first formal naming of streets in Aberdeen:—

> "19th January, 1764.—The said day, the Council appointed the new street leading from the Schoolhill towards the Loch and immediately west of the Tannage Yard to be called from hence in all time coming The Tannerie Street; and the other new street made out by William Littlejohn from the Gallowgate to the Back Causeway The East Street of the Gallowgate. And appointed this Act to be insert as a Domestick in the next "Aberdeen Journal"†

*Soon after Beattie's death in 1803, his friends were allowed to put up a monument to his memory in Drum's Aisle on payment of One Guinea. Like Francis Peacock's, that monument has disappeared.

†Council Register, LXIV., folio of date.

It is curious that of the two streets thus for the first time formally named by the Town Council neither of them retained the official name. "Tannerie Street" did last till the extension of the street in 1808, when it became George Street. But I think the formal name of the other street never was used at all. From the first, it was known as Littlejohn's Street, and as "Littlejohn Street" it will probably remain to the end of the chapter.

A little further along the Gallowgate we reach the Port Hill, so named from the fact that the Gallowgate Port, or gate stood here, near the top of Young Street. The Gallowgate Port stood till 1769. Its fate is decreed in the following ordinance of the Town Council:—

"24th February, 1769—The said day, the Council considering that the different Ports of the town, particularly the Netherkirkgate, Gallowgate, and Justice Ports are great obstructions to carriages of all kinds entering to and going out of town, of which repeated complaints have been made, and also applications for their being removed. The Council, therefore, unaminously agreed that the Justice Port and the Gallowgate Port shall be immediately taken down and removed, and recommended to the Magistrates to cause execute the same accordingly; as also to enquire how far it is practicable to remove the Netherkirkgate Port, and if found practicable to cause take down and remove the same likewise."*

We have already seen that in spite of this decree, the Justice Port was not actually removed till 1787.†

*Council Register, LXIII., fol. 119.

†See *Ante*, p. 29.

The Gallowgate Port was now swept away, however, for we know that in 1778, not quite ten years afterwards, the Town Council disposed and conveyed to John Niven, merchant in Aberdeen, a piece of waste and vacant ground at the Gallowgate-head, upon the east side of the street, "where the Port formerly stood."* So that ancient structure also disappeared, although more than a hundred years before it had been so much esteemed that the King's arms on the outside of it, which had become obliterated, were ordered to be revived.†

Young Street, connecting Gallowgate with the Lochside, is a memorial of a Provost—William Young, of Sheddochsley. He owned ground near the Loch, and was, I think, one of the partners of the company that owned the factory—still standing—at the corner of Gallowgate and Seamount Place. John Ewen, that enterprising personage, whose doings as a Police Commissioner we have already had under view, was a pioneer in the laying out of Young Street. In January, 1806, he informed the Police Commissioners that the Porthill Factory Company had it in view to lay out a street from the Gallowgate-head to the Loch, and got a committee appointed to visit, and report on the scheme. A few days afterwards, the committee reported "that they had met with one of the proprietors of the Porthill Factory, who pointed out to them the

*Council Register, LXIV., fol. 133. This is probably the same John Niven who is said to have put up the figure of the warrior on the Wallace Tower. See *Ante*, p. 71.

†Ibid., LV., fol. 156.

intended improvement by widening and enlarging the passage so to make it a street communicating with John Street." The Board very much approved of the scheme, and their only concern was "that it should be carried speedily into effect," and they directed their treasurer to write the company "requesting information how soon they thought they would be able to begin."*

*Register of Police Commissoners, I., f. 378.

CHAPTER VIII

HUTCHEON STREET DISTRICT: BERRYDEN AND ITS MONUMENTS: CAUSEWAYEND: MOUNTHOOLY: A CHURCH NAME: THE SPITAL: POWIS AND THE POW BURN: A CELEBRATED PAMPHLET: KITTYBREWSTER AS A PERSONAL AND PLACE NAME.

AS we pass northwards from the Gallowgate we find the streets dating largely from the beginning of last century. Nelson Street is one of these. It began to be laid out at the time of Trafalgar, and in 1807 was ready to be feued out in building lots. It was never a very popular street. Judging from John Smith's "Plan" of 1810, no lots seem to have been feued at that date.*

The name of Kingsland Place, near Gerard Street, is a little puzzling. Mr. Alexander Forbes, Albyn Terrace, informs me that when his grandfather built Kingsland House, the feu-duty was payable to King's College, hence, perhaps, King's-land Place. On the other hand, there was a Kingsland Road in London, and as the application of London street names was

*Unfortunately, this Plan of the town, though beautifully executed, is quite unreliable as regards the feus actually built upon at that date. Many feus are shown filled up which were certainly not built upon for years afterwards.

rather in fashion in Aberdeen just then—witness Spring Gardens, just opposite Kingsland Place—the name may have originated in this way.

Gerard Street (not "Gerrard" Street, as it is now spelt), which was formed by 1810, was named after Dr. Alexander Gerard, minister of Greyfriars, and Professor of Theology. He was a noted local personage in his day—chiefly, as one of the "sapient septemviri," the seven professors who were hostile to the 1786 scheme for the union of King's and Marischal Colleges. Catherine Street was laid out on what was known as Tolquhon's Croft, also University ground, in 1806-7. Who Catherine was, has long ago been forgotten, and only a lucky accident can now rediscover.

Hutcheon Street was named after Hugh Hutcheon, advocate, proprietor of part of the lands, and factor for much more of the property in that neighbourhood. The street was formed in the opening years of last century, partly on the lands of Broadford, and in the *Aberdeen Journal* of January 21, 1807, might be seen an intimation that on the 10th March following would be sold "The lands of Broadford and eleventh lot of the lands of Gilcomston adjoining, belonging to the trustees of the deceased Hugh Hutcheon, advocate in Aberdeen." The Hutcheon family had a great deal of the legal business of Aberdeen in their hands in the beginning of last century. The portrait of one of them David Hutcheon, advocate, may be seen to this day in the Medico-Chirurgical Hall, King Street. It was painted and hung there in 1830 "as a mark of respect for his unremitting and courteous services as treasurer and legal adviser (of the Society) for upwards of thirty years."

It is impossible to mention Hutcheon Street without associating with it Berryden, a street name that comes to us from the last quarter of the eighteenth century. At that time the property was acquired by Alexander Leslie, druggist, Broad Street. Advised by his friend, John Ewen, already spoken of, he laid out the grounds of Berryden in rather an artistic way and erected those whimsical brick structures that are still a source of quiet wonder in the neighbourhood.* Alexander Leslie's man of business was Hugh Hutcheon, advocate, of Hutcheon Street, but he was more than that, for we learn from the Aberdeen Register of Marriages that on 29th November, 1795, Hugh Hutcheon, advocate, married Helen Leslie, daughter of Alexander Leslie, merchant, of Berryden. Leslie died in 1799, and Hugh Hutcheon, his son-in-law, survived him only till 1806, when his property, as above noted, was advertised for sale.†

*I have already told the detail story of Berryden and these structures in the article, "Berryden and some of its Associations," in the Book of Powis, 1906.

†A gravestone in the churchyard of Battle, near Hastings, has this inscription—

TO THE MEMORY OF
THOMAS LESLIE OF BERRYDEN,
IN THE COUNTY OF ABERDEEN,
WHO DIED AT BATTLE ON THE 8TH SEPT., 1833,
AGED 61.
ERECTED BY HIS NIECE JANE HINDMAN.

S. N. and Q. in *Aberdeen Weekly Journal*, 24th May, 1910.

Returning eastwards by Hutcheon Street we reach Causewayend. The meaning of this name is quite obvious. It is the end of the causeway—that is, the end of the made street, the Gallowgate. I do not think the name is very old, not older than the seventeenth century, probably. Sir Alexander Hay's mortification for the up-keep of the old Bridge of Don included a feu-duty of thirty-three shillings and four pennies from the "Calsey Croft," which lay just outside the Gallowgate Port, where Causewayend begins.* The date of that is 1605, and the name Causewayend, as a street name, is later than that. Previously, it was merely a country road, spoken of as the "common gait," leading to the burgh. Causewayends are common in other Scottish towns, having arisen in the same way, and many readers will be aware that it is the name of a railway station on one of the North British branch lines near Bo'ness.

Calsayseat Road in this quarter was so named by the Town Council, on the suggestion of Messrs. Jenkins & Marr, architects, acting for the proprietor, in April, 1884. It is appropiately named, for it is laid out on the piece of land known of old as the Calsey Croft. In 1849 Hugh Fraser Leslie of Powis received from the Town Council a charter confirming to him "All and whole that portion of the Land of the Commonty of the Burgh of Aberdeen called Calsey Seat."† In the early description of the

*Mortifications under the charge of the Provost, Magistrates, and Town Council, 1849, p. 34.

†Charter of confirmation, now held by the Great North of Scotland Railway Company.

Calsayseat (latterly known as Split-the-Wind).

Site now occupied by Powis Parish Church, built 1895.

property we are told that the boundary crosses "the Sleek or Den, called Kattie Brewster eastward by the Lands called Broadford or Crooked Myres, belonging to George Dingwall, late Baillie in Aberdeen, as the same is divided from the same Lands of Calsey Seat by ditches, fail dykes, and stone dykes, and the ends of the yeards belonging to Calsey Seat till it comes to the Causeway that goes from that to the Gallowgate-head.*

There is one street in this locality the name of which is most difficult to explain. I mean Mounthooly. Since the middle of the eighteenth century the name has been variously spelt Mount Hooley, Mount Heillie, Mountheely, Mount Hillie, and again Mount Hooley, but there is no special significance in that. Then, as a street name, Mounthooly comes, in the last instance, from Mounthooly Croft, which lay slightly beyond where John Knox Parish Church now stands, and formed one of the zone of crofts of land within the town's inner marches. But that does not help us much in getting at the meaning of the name.

One helpful circumstance is that the name is not a local one, confined to Aberdeen. You have a Mounthooly in Roxburghshire, another in Linlithgowshire, a third in Buchan, near Pitsligo, and the street in Peterhead now known as James Street was formerly known as Mounthooly.† There are three Mounthoolies in Caithness-shire. One is in Wick, a mount on

*The same, extracted by Mr. George Davidson, General Manager of the Company.

†Mr. J. F. Tocher, Peterhead, finds this from investigation of the Town's records.

which it is said the church at one time stood; another at Kirk, where a chapel stood, but the name here is said on good authority to have been borrowed from the third Mounthooly (or halie) in the Parish of Dunnet.* There is a Mounthooly in Lerwick, but it has been shown to be an importation.† There is also a Mounthooly Lane in Kirkwall, where a church dedicated to St. Olaf stood.

Now, all this means that the name is evidently a general descriptive designation, applied at first in a strictly descriptive way as we have seen happened in the case of our earliest street names.

In this view one suggestion as to the meaning of the name is that it is Gaelic, and may be Monadh Chuile, "hill with the corner," comparable to Knockhoolie, or Knockhillie, at Colvend.‡ Such an explanation might conceivably suit the Mounthooly at Aberdeen, and twenty other hills in the district, but it may not suit all the places so named; in any case, there must be an enormous number of "hills with

*Particulars kindly sent me by Rev. D. Beaton, Wick, author of the History of Caithness-shire, and other works.

†Rev. A. J. Campbell, Lerwick, gives the following amusing particulars with regard to it—"Shortly after the Reform Bill the authorities of Lerwick came to the conclusion that the old street names, Kirk Close, Tait's Close, Baker's Close, etc., were vulgar, and ought to be altered to something more respectable. At the foot of the Baker's Close lived and worked one William Sievwright, who hailed from Aberdeen—an antiquary thinks from Mounthooly itself—and the name Mounthooly was adopted on his suggestion."

‡Johnston, Falkirk, in his Place Names of Scotland, p. 225.

corners" in Scotland that are not named Mounthooly, and so one may safely entertain a grave doubt as to this suggested derivation.

A more plausible suggestion is that the "hoolie," or "hillie" in the name is simply a pleonasm, a repetition of the "Mount," as happens occasionally, and as we have seen happened in the case of the Pow-burn. And yet this explanation is far from satisfactory, and it gives no light or reason why the pleonasm should occur just in the case of those particular hills, and not in any number of hills in their neighbourhood.

No, we must find a particular reason why the name was applied in every instance, and we do not find that in either of the suggestions above noted. My present conviction is that the "halie," "hely," or "heilie" in the name is simply the ordinary spelling in use in the middle centuries for "holy," and that the name is the Holy Mount, meaning that it was Church land, or that a church or chapel stood there.

This we have seen to be the case in these instances where the name is indigenous in the far north. It was certainly the case in Aberdeen. In the twelfth century the hospital dedicated to St. Peter was founded in what we now know as the Spital at Mounthooly, and the chapel that afterwards existed in connection with it would probably be sufficient, of itself, to give the designation "halie" to lands or the hill in the immediate neighbourhood. Then, in point of fact, there was a piece of land there known as the holy-lande, meaning ground belonging to the church. It is named for the first time, so far as I know, in 1492. In a charter of that year one Andrew Ancroft a burgess of Aberdeen, sold an annual rent of twenty shillings to Mr. Symon Dods, said rents to be drawn from his two crofts of land lying on the north side of the town—one of which was "the penny croft,"

> "and my other croft or land extending from the top of the hill downwards to the holylande."*

We can hardly doubt that in this we have the true origin of the phrase in "Mountheilie" of the later centuries, and the familiar street name of our own time.

The continuation of Mounthooly as a street is Spital, and, as with all Spitals throughout Scotland, it perpetuates the memory of an Hospital, or Hospice, in that quarter. Says Pennant, in his "Tour" of 1772:—

> "In many parts of the Highlands were Hospitia for the reception of travellers, called by the Scotch 'Spittles,' or Hospitals; the same were usual in Wales where they are styled 'Yspitty,' and in both places were maintained by the religious houses, as similar asylums are to this day supported in many parts of the Alps."†

Cosmo Innes, who understood the matter better than Pennant did, puts it rather more pointedly:—

> "Hospitals very slenderly endowed, were very numerous (in Scotland), At the gates of towns, at the riverside,

*"et de uno alio meo crofto seu terra extendente a vertice montis deorsum usque ad le helylande"—Registrum Epis., Aberd., I., p. 332. In Mr. P. J. Anderson's Plan of the Crofts the Lang Rig intervenes between the Mounthooly Croft and the Holylands.

†Pennant's Tour, I., p. 118.

where a boat was placed, beside the ferry, on the mountain pass—were hospitals for the reception of the poor and pilgrims, for the safety of travellers, for the sick, especially for those afflicted with the scourge of leprosy. They are called Hospitals—Spital—Domus Dei—Maison Dieu—Lazar House—Domus Leprosorum. The foundation consisted generally of a maintenance for two or three brethren (friars, that is) who devoted themselves to the service of the sick and poor."*

The Hospital which is commemorated in our street name "Spital," was founded by Bishop Matthew De Kininmond in the later years of the twelfth century. It was dedicated to St. Peter, and was designed for the reception and support of poor and infirm persons, and was maintained by, among other things, the rents of certain crofts in the neighbourhood, afterwards distinguished by the name of Spital-lands. Afterwards, in 1434, a chapel was added by a charter granted by Bishop de Lychtoun, the builder of St. Machar Cathedral.† In due time the site of both Hospital and Chapel was included in what is now St. Peter's Cemetery.

Perhaps it is going rather beyond our subject of street names, but one is tempted to note in passing the name "Powis" just beyond the Spital—which, indeed, gives the name to Powis Terrace near Kittybrewster. As "Pow" signifies in Gaelic a pool, or stream, so "Powis" we may take to mean originally

*Cosmo Innes. Lectures on Sootch Legal Antiquities, pp. 172-3.

†See the charter signed by the Chapter of the Cathedral, Registrum Epis. Aberdonensis, I., p. 232.

the Burn Lands. The name was continued down to the outlet of the Pow-burn near the North Pier, where that outlet was known as the Pow-creek, afterwards shortened to "Pocra," as we know it in our own day.*

Near Powis Terrace is Leslie Terrace, also laid out on the lands formerly owned by Hugh Leslie of Powis. The name of that gentleman recalls at once his celebrated pamphlet of 1807, "Hot Pressed or the Doctors Outwitted," in which he so assailed certain University Professors and leading citizens that on the application of the Procurator Fiscal, the Magistrates ordered its seizure and destruction. Whereupon Mr. Leslie, with Imlay, the printer of the pamphlet, commenced actions for damages against the Magistrates in the Court of Session. He suffered grievous defeat, for the Court held that the publication contained matter of the most scandalous and libellous nature against the defenders both in their private and public chatacter. The pamphlet seems a paltry enough production nowadays, and serves to show how unwholesome the local atmosphere could easily become only a century ago.†

Near Powis Terrace, we have Bedford Road, in which the entrance to Powis House is situated. Bed-

*See *Ante*. The Pow-creek gave the name to the Pow-creek Croft, a piece of ground that lay east of the Castle-hill, which was feued out in 1794. For many years the Pow-creek was simply a sewer for the north side of the town. See Report of the Proceedings in the Committee of the House of Commons in regard to the Aberdeen Harbour Bill, 1839.

†The pamphlet, which is now very scarce, may be consulted in the Local Collection of the Public Library.

ford Road used to be known as Erskine Road—reminiscent of Erskine of Pittodrie (hence also Pittodrie Place) a former landed proprietor of the neighbourhood. In 1884, the Town Council changed the name, as it led to confusion wtth Erskine Street—which was very reasonable—but why the name Bedford Road was chosen no one seems able to explain.

We are now in the Kittybrewster district, and although no street actually carries that name, it is far too interesting as a familiar local designation in use for centuries to be passed over.

Not long ago, it was suggested by a responsible Aberdeen writer that the legend of "Kitty Brewster," as a personality, was invented by the late Mr. William Cadenhead in his verses written fully twenty years ago, and embodied in his posthumous volume, "Ingatherings." That is far from being the case. William Cadenhead himself knew better. In point of fact, he had actual history in view when he wrote the lines telling that "Kitty Brewster" kept a tavern

"Out on the road to Hilton."

On 9th April, 1754, the Town Council of Aberdeen passed an act "for repairing the Road twixt the Town and Katy Browster's Feu on the Hilton Road."* That seems very conclusive, and one would be justified in supposing from it that a person of the name of Kitty Brewster actually held a feu there at that time, or about that time. But if one supposed anything of the kind, he would be wrong. The name goes very much further back. George Cadenhead, in his

*Council Register, vol., 1753-63, fol. 21.

"Aberdeen Burgh Territories," quoted a record of the town's boundaries, of date 2nd August, 1673, telling that on the north side of the town the boundary kept "the said gate (or road) to ane merch stone in the Den called Kettiebrauster."* Even this is not the first. The boundaries are previously described in the Burgh Registers, on 15th June, 1615, where the same words are used in connection with a riding of the marches, stating that the boundary went on "theirfra, keipand the gett to ane merche stane in the den callit Kittiebrouster."† Obviously, this is not the beginning, for it is spoken of so familiarly in the record that it must have been in use for a long time prior even to 1615.

From this point backward I have not found "Kittybrewster" as a personal name, and I have formed the impression that it is not a personal name at all, but a name descriptive of use. In very early days, the land near the Loch of Old Aberdeen (which lay in the hollow between the Chanonry and where the railway now runs) was known as the "Browster Land." In the Register of the Bishopric occurs this entry of the year 1376 in a Confirmation of the Bishop over ground near the Chanonry (rendered)—

> "All that piece of land of ours lying between the manse of the prebend of Deer on the north, and our land which is now called the Brousterlande (et terram nostram que nunc vocatur le Brousterlande) on the south, beginning

*Sketch of the Territorial History of Aberdeen; Trans. Abdn. Philos. Soc., I., 87.

†Council Register, II., f. 326.

at the head of the common highway which goes by the Chanonry to the Church on the east, and extends to the Loch on the west."*

We have the same thing again, in the year 1431, where the ground is similarly described as "our land which is now called the Broustar Land" (terram nostram que nunc vocatur le Broustarlande). The second entry descriptive of the property is simply, of course, a copy of the first, as is still customary in such documents, so the "now" in 1431 has no significance. But if the description of 1376 be really—as it seems to be—the first of the kind, then the "now" is important as taking us to the beginning of the name of the Browster Land.

All this does not prove to a demonstration that in the "Browster Land" we have the origin of the name "Kittybrewster." That may come later. Meantime, it seems more than a coincidence that "the Den called Kettiebrauster" in the seventeenth century should be near by, or actually on the "Browster" Land of the fourteenth century.

What was meant by the Browster Land is not very difficult to see. We know that the Bishop had a brew-house in Old Aberdeen, as had most other houses of any consequence, even in the city of Aberdeen, down to the eighteenth century. I suppose the browster land was the land from which the grain was set apart for brewing purposes. And perhaps, it is here, after all, that we get at the origin of the legend which associated the "brewster" in the name with the keeper of a tavern.

*Registrum Episcopatus Aberdonensis, I., p. 193.

CHAPTER IX

THE LOCHLANDS: CORRECTION WYND: WINDMILL BRAE: PROVOST LEYS AND THE MAKING OF UNION STREET: FERRYHILL STREETS: JOHN CRAB AND THE CRABSTONE: ARCHIBALD SIMPSON, ARCHITECT, AND THE CRAIBSTONE STREETS: WEST END STREET NAMES.

RETURNING from Kittybrewster towards the heart of the city, by Gallowgate, we turn down from the last named thoroughfare by St. Paul Street. This street is named from the still existing St. Paul's Episcopal Chapel, founded in 1720, which stood there, accordingly, for over 120 years before St. Paul Street was laid out in 1842. It was laid out partly on the site of the Vennel, which had come to be looked on as perhaps the worst "slum" in Aberdeen. This, so far as I know, is the earliest authoritative mention of this improvement—from the proceedings of the Police Commissioners:—

"4th August, 1841.—Mr. Webster reported on the part of the Finance and Street Committees that he had seen Mr. Jopp, advocate, in reference to a proposal to form a new street from Gallowgate via the Vennel to Loch Street, and that the only obstacle to doing so arose in consequence of Mrs. Wilson, the proprietor of two of the houses, refusing to sell her property at a reasonable price; it was therefore proposed that the Board shall make an offer of £120, that sum being considered the full value of the property, and failing her accepting the said sum, or agreeing to refer the value to arbiters mutually chosen within twenty-one days after the offer is made, the Board shall apply to the Sheriff to summon a jury for the purpose of fixing the the price of said property, in terms of the 95th Section of the Act of Parliament."*

The little lane that connects St. Paul Street and Upperkirkgate, known as Drum's Lane, is older than St. Paul Street, but is not so ancient as might be supposed. It was formed in the year 1800, and took its name from the fact that it was constructed partly on the garden ground of what was known as Lady Drum's Hospital—the dwelling of widows and spinsters for whose maintenance Lady Irvine of Drum mortified with the Town Council 3000 merks Scots in 1633.

George Street we have already slightly touched upon, but we note it here as taking us among the group of streets laid out in what was known a century ago as the Lochlands. The part that was known for some years as Tannery Street began as a small street in 1754, when the Town Council bought certain tenements and yard belonging to a Mrs. Urquhart for £1000 Scots, in order to open a new street from Schoolhill and Upperkirkgate, below the Port, to the

*Register of Police Commissoners, VII., f. 250. The Vennel was finally cleared away in 1842. "We are glad to observe that the whole of the buildings extending from Gallowgate to Loch Street, on the site formerly occupied by the Vennel, have now been removed. . . . . . The line of the new street, which from its neighbourhood to the Chapel is to be called St. Paul Street, has, we learn, been laid off." *Aberdeen Journal*, 25th May, 1842.

Loch-eye. Soon afterwards, a feu was given off on the east side of the new street to the Tannery Company, at an annual feu-duty of £27, and the Town Council ordained in 1764 that the new street should be known thenceforth as Tannery Street.

It was towards the end of the eighteenth century that an enterprising citizen, James Staats Forbes, a china and general merchant in Queen Street, turned his attention to the feuing out of the Lochlands. In 1783, accordingly, this stretch of ground, which yielded crops of grass chiefly for the feeding of "ky and other bestiall," was put up to public roup, on leases of 999 years, conform to a feuing plan drawn out by Colin Innes, land surveyor. The articles of roup gave details as to the various "lots," and the names given to the prospective streets, as follows:—

> "The first, which runs in a line with Tannery Street, is to be called now, and in all time coming, George Street; the street or lane which leads from Tannery Street, round by the Back Yard to the back gate of Robert Gordon's Hospital, is to be called Crooked Lane; the street or lane leading from the back gate of Robert Gordon's Hospital to the Infirmary to be called Hospital Row [afterwards made part of St. Andrew Street]; the street which runs nearly in a line with the north gate of Robert Gordon's Hospital, to be called Charlotte Street; the street which runs from the said north entry of Robert Gordon's Hospital towards the Loch, to be called St. Andrew's Street; and the other street which runs from Rotten Holes [at Gilcomston Steps] to the Loch, parallel to St. Andrew's Street, to be called John Street."*

* The Loch of Aberdeen, by the late Mr. James Rettie, in the Book of Saint George's-in-the-West, 1892. This is the most

By this scheme of new streets, George Street was carried northward to connect with the Inverurie turnpike. On the line of it was the old "Ford Gate," or Ford Road, leading to the "broad ford" across the north end of the Loch, or the stream that entered the Loch at the north end. Jopp's Lane was formed at the same time, and took its name from Andrew Jopp, advocate, who was agent for Staats Forbes in the feuing of the Lochlands.

Meantime, George Street and Tannery Street had no outlet at the town end, except by Upperkirkgate on the one hand, and Schoolhill on the other. On the completion of Union Street in 1805, a movement began to take shape, first with the Town Council, and afterwards with the Police Commissoners, for having this whole line of street carried in to connect with Union Street. The result was the opening of St. Nicholas Street, one of the most happily named of the newer streets of Aberdeen. Its formation obliterated the old Dubbie Raw, and led to the widening and improvement of Tannery Street, a name that also now disappeared, for the improved and extended thoroughfare became George Street all the way from St. Nicholas Street to North Broadford.

In passing from St. Nicholas Street stationwards, we give little attention nowadays to Correction Wynd, for it is now more than ever a by-street. For many years it was known simply as a "common vennel,"

accurate and interesting story of the Loch of Aberdeen that has ever been written. Mr. Rettie devoted himself for some time to a special study of the subject.

but it took its present name from the Correction House established there under a patent obtained from Charles I., in 1636. It was a sort of work-house for the making of cloth, whither offenders were sent, but it never was a prosperous undertaking, either as a private enterprise or as worked under the management of the town. It was discontinued in 1711.*

When Union Street was carried over Correction Wynd by the still existing bridge, an agitation arose among the residents in the Green for an access to Union Street by a stair at Correction Wynd Bridge. This was in 1806. The idea then was that the stair should ascend at the south end of the arch—from the Green; and even in 1818, when contracts were ultimately taken for the construction of the stair, this was the accepted plan. Before the work was begun, the plans were so far alterated as to provide for the stair being built at the north end of the arch, where it still continues in use.

We need not stop to discuss the name of the Green, for I have already had an opportunity of dealing with it in detail.† I may only say here that fuller inquiry has but deepened the conclusion come to on the facts in the small work mentioned that the Green never was the burgh green of Aberdeen, but was always a street outside the town, and simply led to the well known public Green by the Denburn-side.

*For the contract for the erection of the Correction House, 8th February, 1636, see Extracts ftom the Aberdeen Burgh Registers (Record Society) I., p. 102.

†In The Green and its Story, 1903.

It was, in fact, as the early charters still have it, "Vicus Viridis," the Green-gait, the road or way to the Green.*

We pass on to Windmill Brae, which takes its name from the windmill that stood near the top for many years, where Crown Street now is. Baillie Walter Robertson, a worthy historian of Aberdeen, tells, in 1685, that in the preceding years, under the Provostship of Sir George Skene of Fintray,

> "there is a comely and strong windmill newly built, at the south entry to the town, which is and may be of eminent use to the town."

The name of Crown Street belongs to a group of fanciful names dating from the early years of last century, including Diamond Street, Silver Street, Golden Square, and so forth. They were all laid out by the Hammermen Corporation of the Incorporated Trades, who, in providing for the junction of Crown Street with Union Street, in 1806, diverted the street slightly westward to avoid the necessity of bridging Windmill Brae, hence the rather unsightly bend at the top of Crown Street still.†

*It is curious to note that as recently as July of this year, Mr. Charles Masefield, author of "Staffordshire" in the English series of County Histories, writes pointing out to me that the Greengate in Stafford formerly led to the old Green outside the walls. It seems an exactly parallel case.

†Golden Square and adjoining streets were laid out mainly on what was known as the Longlands. They were completed about 1820. In July, 1821, the "essay" prescribed for a candidate for entry to the Hammermen Craft was "a key to the well in Golden Square." At the same date legal proceedings

In laying out this group of streets—which are still, after a century, quite a credit to the city—the Hammermen Corporation acted in concert with the civic authorities, especially with the New Street Trustees, who had in hand the laying out of Union Street. And as bearing on that, and the arrangements carried out for the proper design of these streets west of Union Bridge, I think it will be interesting to quote the following letter from Provost Leys to the Deacon of the craft, showing the care exercised in details in carrying out this important undertaking :

"Aberdeen, 23rd February, 1804.

"Sir—For some time past the New Street Trustees and their Committee have had under consideration what plan would be most appropriate to be laid down for the buildings to be erected along both sides of Union Street west of the Denburn, and in doing so it has occurred to them that it will be for the interest of all concerned that the restrictions to be imposed upon the different proprietors and feuars should be as few as possible.

"With this view, they propose that the only limitations in regard to the buildings shall be that the front houses between each opening, or cross street, which may hereafter be made out shall form one compartment, and shall be of the same height of five wall number of floors and pitch of roof, and that the whole shall be built of well-dressed granite stone.

"They also propose that the front walls shall be retired eight feet from each side of the street, so as to form a sunk floor or area of that breadth, having an iron railing

had to be threatened in order to induce the feuars to pay up their share of the expense of the garden railing in Golden Square which still stands.

Ferryhill Mills.

Of which the burn gives the name to Millburn Street, *c.* 1840.

towards the street, which will be found not only very convenient and useful but will tend much to beautify the street itself.

"The particular plans of the fronts of each compartment, and the situation of the cross streets, can easily be adjusted between the trustees and the proprietors and others concerned.

"I flatter myself these proposals are so reasonable that no person can have the least objection to agree to them. I have, therefore, thought proper to make you acquainted therewith. . . . . I at the same time beg leave to mention that by laying down Union Street ten feet wider towards the south than was originally intended, the extent and value of the building areas belonging to the trustees will be considerably reduced.* They would, therefore, be willing to feu or purchase some of the small pieces of ground belonging to your Corporation situated between those areas and the Windmill Brae at such reasonable price or feu duty as may be agreed to.

"I am, sir, your most obedient servant,

"THOMAS LEYS, Provost."†

As we pass down Crown Street, one or two street names—among others of obvious meaning—claim attention. Marywell Street, projected in 1809, was laid out by the Shoemaker Trade on the Marywell Croft. The well, dedicated to St. Mary, from which the ground took its name, was situated near the foot of Gordon Street, behind what was for many years a tobacco pipe manufactory.

*There is a tradition that Union Street was made ten feet wider than was originally intended by the surreptitious removal of the pegs, backward, during the night. The above—apart from other proofs—disposes of the story.

†From the archives of the Hammermen Incorporation, Trinity Hall.

Affleck Street was also laid out by the Shoemaker Incorporation, and they named it after the Deacon of their craft, Andrew Affleck, Convener of the Trades in 1826-7. Convener Affleck was a well-known public personage in his day. He had a shoemaker's shop in Union Street, between Shiprow and Adelphi, and dwelt for a good many years at No. 2 Affleck Place. His brother, James Affleck, as formerly remarked, owned the well-known Affleck's Tavern, in Burnett's Close. Convener Affleck's benevolence in the east end of the town was almost proverbial. It is probably not so well-known that, while a member of the George Street U. P. Congregation, he presented to the church, in 1824, the first gas lamp that was used in Aberdeen.* Convener Affleck's generosity was exemplified in a more literary way in connection with the Incorporated Trades. Dr. Guild's mortification of property to the Trades was translated from the original Latin by Rev. John Bisset, the Patron, and in 1825 the document was printed at the expense of Deacon Andrew Affleck "For the Information of the Young Members of the Seven Incorporations."†

Beyond Affleck Street, we have Millburn Street, so named from the stream that ran along here from the Ferryhill Mill Dam to the Dee.

One puzzling street name still exists in this neighbourhood. Every now and again one sees the

*This curious fact I owe to the late Ex-Baillie George Walker, who was latterly the oldest surviving member of that congregation.

†A copy of this interesting little work may be consulted in the reference department of the Aberdeen Public Library.

question asked in the newspapers—what is the origin of the name College Street. The name arises from the fact that Marischal College held property here, in the neighbourhood of Poynernook. Some light is thrown on this by the following entry in the Burgh Registers :—

> "10th December, 1789—The said day, the Council having heard the petition of the Principal and Professors of the Marischal College, craveing liberty to erect a bridge over the Denburn, a little below the Bow Bridge opposite to the Bulwark, for giving the petitioners more easy access to lands belonging to them on the opposite side of said Burn, which they intend to feu out, in case the same should be deemed necessary by the purchasers of said feus."*

Moving west of Crown Street, we come to Dee Street, rather a curious name, it may be thought, to find so far from the Dee. It is, however, the second of the name. The original Dee Street ran near the river where the Joint Station now stands, and when the present Dee Street was laid out, about 1806 or 1807, it was named New Dee Street, afterwards Upper Dee Street. When the original street, then known as Lower Dee Street, was obliterated by the incoming of the Denburn Junction Railway in 1867, there was no further need of any distinguishing epithet in the street name.

Adjoining Dee Street is Gordon Street, a street quite without character, and badly engineered from the first, for it may be said to have had neither entrance nor outlet. It was laid out between 1800

*Register of Town Council, LXVI., f. 64.

and 1807, by one Thomas Gordon, a feuar, who gave his name to the street. Speculation arises sometimes as to the identity of this person. In one respect we know whom he was not. An account appeared in the *Aberdeen Observer* in 1831 of the suicide of a person of the name of Gordon, who resided in this street, and the writer of the account went on to say:—"We think it right to state that this man was no relation to the gentleman of the same name, who is proprietor of the street in which he resided." In point of fact, Thomas Gordon was a worthy mason who, without any proper ideas as to street-making, laid out the street which was named after him, and feued off part of it for weaving shops. His son, possessor of the superiority, was Thomas Gordon, of Gordon & Smith, a well-known Union Street merchant for many years.

Further west we touch a series of street names too recent to be historical. Bon-Accord Street, Bon-Accord Square, and Bon-Accord Terrace (now Crescent) date from the twenties of last century, and we may still point to the two last-named streets as distinguished examples of the fine taste of Archibald Simpson, architect, who laid them out for the Tailor Craft of the Incorporated Trades. It is a remarkable circumstance that the noted architect and the Craft fell out, and their relations became so embittered that Simpson was practically dismissed as the Trades' architectural adviser. They came together again afterwards, and Simpson built a house for himself and another for his brother in Bon-Accord Square (now

Nos. 13 and 15) and still later he purchased the house No. 1 East Craibstone Street, in which he died in 1847.

Mention of Craibstone Street reminds us that these streets were formed partly on the Crabstone Croft, a name that suggests many varied historical and personal associations. But we can touch on them only sparingly. John Crab, whose boundary stone gave the name to the quarter, was one of the most remarkable Aberdonians of his time. Originally a Fleming, he performed national service for the Scots at the siege of Berwick in 1319, for it was the stones from his crane that shattered the roof of the English "sow." He afterwards settled in Aberdeen, and acquired property in every other street, as well as in the suburbs. He owned property at Kincorth, and it is from a charter granted in connection with this property that we get our only certain information relative to the existence of a Bridge over the Dee there, in 1384, nearly a century and a half before the founding of the present bridge.* He was a Baillie of the town in 1343, and one of the Commissioners from Aberdeen to the Scots Parliament in 1365 and 1367.† By that time he had rendered further national service by becoming (1357) one of the sureties for payment of the ransom of David II., the unfortunate Scots King who was taken prisoner at the Battle of Neville's

*See Registrum Epis. Aberd., II., p. 286, also article by present writer, "The Bridges of Aberdeen," in John Knox Bazaar Book, 1910.

†Exchequer Rolls of Scotland, I., Preface, etc.

Cross.* John Crab acquired among his other possessions the property near Bucksburn afterwards, and still, known as Crab's-toun (or Craibstone), and he owned the parcel of ground in the town's inner marches known as the Crabstone Croft, where the boundary stone, which still carries the name of Crab's Stone, stood,† and where the great Crabstone rout of the Aberdonians by Montrose's wild Highlanders took place in 1644. It was in this neighbourhood that the streets so familiar to us as East and West Craibstone Streets were laid out, and they carry on historical and personal memories of a quality that attaches to few other street names in the city.

On the other side of Union Street the street names are all comparatively recent. Crimond Place, which dates, like all of them there, from the early years of last century, is a difficult name. I suspect it arises from the circumstance that the street was laid out partly on ground at the back of the Laird of Crimon-mogate's house in Union Street, now the home of the Northern Club. Huntly Street, too, is puzzling, but I have little doubt it is named after the Marquis of Huntly, who was a great figure in Aberdeen life at the time of its formation, 1818-1820. When Huntly Street was formed, Summer Street was still known as the Summer Road, the name it had borne

*Cosmo Innes—Lectures on Scotch Legal Antiquities, p. 107; Marwick—Charters relating to Edinburgh, I., p. 19.

†Crab's Stone is still in existence—at the stable door in Hardgate of a West Craibstone Street house. It is surely worthy of being better cared for.

since 1771, when the Gilcomston Chapel of Ease was put up there chiefly to accommodate the quarrying population that had sprung up in the neighbourhood of Loanhead and Northfield.

Three other street names in that quarter are associated with Gilcomston Chapel and its most notable minister, namely, Kidd Lane (now Kidd Street), Minister Lane, and Chapel Street. We are here, too, into the region of fanciful names—Thistle Street and Rose Street, Victoria Street and Albert Street, of the last of which Osborne Place and Hanover Street were perhaps an inevitable sequel. A more interesting street name in that quarter has disappeared in recent years—Henry Street. It carried the name of George Henry, Provost of the city in 1850-53. Provost Henry, who died in March, 1867, was a very quaint personage, as would be understood from the tradition of him that he was the last person in Aberdeen to wear powdered hair.*

Union Street was not always so named to its furthest limits. The upper or westmost part, as many will easily remember, was known up to about twenty years ago as Union Place. It was constructed, in connection with Holburn Street, out of Commutation Road funds, at the beginning of last century, and up

*It will be remembered that Henry Street, when formed, was carried up to the boundary wall of Bridewell—so named after the famous London prison. It was constructed under an Act of Parliament obtained in 1802, and was the prison of Aberdeen till 1868, when it was abandoned on the completion of the new prison in Lodge Walk.

till very recently had a smaller class of houses than Union Street proper. When the Town Council resolved, 17th February, 1890, that the name Union Place should be abolished, and the whole line of street known thenceforth as Union Street, the owners and residents in Union Place, for some reason, objected to the change. A few of the old Union Place houses are still standing, most of them having their lower fronts transformed into modern business premises, and the building may still be seen to which this intimation of 1807 refers :—

> "Shop to Let—In that new House just finished in Union Street [and Union Place] corner of Chapel Street. . . . . As the great south road, from Union Street to Bridge of Dee, is expected to be opened in a few months, forming a junction with the Deeside and Skene turpike roads, all passing by the said premises, it will soon be one of the most centrical situations for business on that side of the town."*

The "great south road" here spoken of is what became, fifteen years afterwards, Holburn Road, and is now Holburn Street. It is a little odd that this street passes over the Howburn (*i.e.* Howe Burn—hence Howburn Place, etc.) and possibly that may have suggested the name of the famous London street.

Union Grove the name of the long line of street extending from Holburn Street to Forest Avenue, perpetuates the name of the residential property of Union Grove owned by Provost Hadden and his family for many years. The street is laid out partly

***Aberdeen Journal*, 11th March, 1807.

on the grounds of Union Grove and over the site of the dam that supplied the Upper Justice Mill for centuries. It takes us into the heart of the Ashley district that has been covered with new streets within the last generation, whose names are all too recent to call for explanation here.

CHAPTER X

THE MUTTON BRAE: BLACK'S BUILDINGS: GEORGE JAMESONE AND HIS GARDEN: HARDWEIRD: ST. JOHN'S WELL: JACK'S BRAE: A STRANGE PUBLISHING HOUSE: THE GILCOMSTON DAM: "HOPE STREET": THE CRAIGIE LOANINGS.

THE Schoolhill was more a suburb than a street of Aberdeen in the old days. Beyond St. Nicholas Church, up till about the time of the Reformation, little was to be seen except town's commonty, through which a track led to the hamlet of Gilcomstoun. But three institutions there, all connected with the Church, gave character and name to the locality. One of these was the Grammar School, which was situated in the Schoolhill for nearly seven centuries that we know of, till its removal to its present site in Skene Street in 1863.* The second of these notable institutions was the Sang School, a continuous adjunct of St. Nicholas Church from the middle of the fourteenth century till it was discontinued in 1749.† The third institution familiar in

*The present Grammar School was erected out of the Common Good at a cost of £13,000. The old school must have been for long an extremely small building, since we are told by Baillie Walter Robertson that in 1657-60 it was "greatly lengthened and enlarged, as it now stands."

†See, for the story of the Sang School, Historical Aberdeen, pp. 49-53.

the Schoolhill was the Conventual Buildings and Chapel of the Black Friars. The site of these buildings is now occupied by the Art Gallery; and it was over part of the Monastery garden ground that Blackfriars Street was laid out in the end of the eighteenth century.

I wish I could explain the meaning of Mutton Brae, that curious street name that ceased when the Brae itself was obliterated by the making of the Schoolhill Viaduct in 1883. In a small book of mine,* I ventured to discuss the probable origin of this name, and a critic in a national periodical airily put the matter right by the suggestion that it was from the Anglo-Saxon *mot*, a meeting, and that probably it was a meeting-place in ancient times. It was an admirable example of the purely academic way of explaining our place names. In point of fact, the Mutton Brae never was a meeting-place in ancient or modern times, and the name is not even ancient, for it is not to be found earlier than the middle of the eighteenth century. And Anglo-Saxon place names were not being applied after 1750.† In discussing such names, we must know not merely the philology of the subject, but the history and topography of the locality as well before we can arrive at anything like certainty.

*Historical Aberdeen, p. 124.

†One helpful thing about the name is that it is not local. There is a farm named Mutton Brae in Fintray, near Kinmuck, and there is another in the parish of Auchreddie, New Deer. Doubtless there are others.

Woolmanhill is the centre of quite a group of interesting street names, for it is at the heart of an ancient suburb of the city. Its own name used to be often spelt "Womanhill," which led such a well-informed person as Gordon of Straloch, famed as an accurate topographer, to suppose that it had some special association with women. But the erroneous spelling arose in a perfectly natural way from the Aberdeen pronunciation of Woolmanhill as "Woo'-manhill," a quite sufficient indication of the ancient use of the place as the site of the wool market of the burgh.

The Woolmanhill of to-day has in the middle of it a wide triangular space which has some historical interest for us. Prior to 1756 it was simply commonty, the Infirmary having been set up on the verge of it a few years before. At the date mentioned it was resolved to deal with the ground as follows:

> "12th February, 1756—The said day, the (Town) Council agrees to expose to Publick Roup and Sale the two following Pieces of ground, viz.,—That triangular Piece of ground near the Infirmary, opposite the South Gate of the Infirmary, whereon the Middings are laid, being a part of the Town's Commonty, to be feued out conform to a Plan or Draught thereof to be seen at the Clerk's Chamber; as also the old Walls at the entry to the Poor's Hospital," etc.*

The piece of ground was duly feued out, and four small houses—one of them a Custom House—stood there for many years. In 1838, the Infirmary Managers having bought up the old properties, the

*Council Register, LXII., f. 115.

houses were cleared away and the place where they stood was added to the street.*

Along the south side of Woolmanhill runs a line of oldish houses known as Black's Buildings. They bear the name of the first proprietor, James Black, wine merchant, Willowbank. The first of them was built in 1798, and the last about 1830, and all came into the market on the sale of Black's sequestrated estate in 1843. Black was one of the best known citizens of the 'thirties of last century, very fond of good company, like so many in his time, and much associated with the convivialities of the community before he came to grief. He died, I think, about 1850. The first idea we get of the feuing of this ground is contained in the following statements by the new Police Commissioners:

"14th May, 1798—The Committee appointed to view the ground on which James Black, merchant, intends to build opposite to the Infirmary South Gate, reported that they had viewed said ground, and are of opinion that if Mr. Black will consent to build on the westmost ground first, and to round off both corners of his house, agreeable to the idea of the Committee, and by direction and at the sight of the Overseer, he might be indulged to secure his house according to the Draught laid before the Commissioners."†

From Woolmanhill, we pass into Spa Street—so named from the Well of Spa, the most celebrated well

*It is said that it was in one of these houses in the Woolmanhill that John Hill Burton was born in 1809. The old houses had become quite ruinous by 1838, and were only cleared away on repeated protests by the neighbouring residents.

†Minutes of Police Commissioners, vol. I., f. 146.

in the Aberdeen district, and thence into Upper Denburn, formerly known as Gilcomston. The name "Gilcomston" I have already had occasion to discuss.* It need only be said here that it does not refer to a "stone," as is sometimes supposed, but to a "toun," or hamlet, just like Ruthrieston, otherwise "Ruadristoun," near the Bridge of Dee. Both carry names of Highland chieftains, neighbours of Aberdeen—one the name of Ruadri, Mormaer of Mar, and the other Gillecolm, son of one Muredach, or Murdoch, a contemporary of Ruadri in the twelfth century.

One can hardly regret the disappearance of a long-familiar name, Garden Nook Close, from the Upper Denburn, for the place needed to be swept away. Yet the name was interesting, for it was the only memorial that was left of the pleasure garden laid out in the Woolmanhill, near the Well of Spa, by George Jamesone, the famous portrait painter. It is far from creditable to Aberdeen that there is no adequate public memorial in his birthplace of this eminent man—the first portrait painter of native genius in the country.

On the other side of Upper Denburn we have "Hardweird," a street name quite as puzzling as our old friends Mounthooly and Mutton Brae. The name comes in the last instance from the Hardweird Croft, but again that scarcely helps us as to the meaning of the name. We have one-half of the name in that of another street, the Hardgate, which just means the hard or made road; and we used to have the other

*See Historical Aberdeen, pp. 142-143, where the name and history of Gilcomston are dealt with in some detail.

half of the name in that of the Sillieweird Croft, which was a neighbouring croft of ground to the Hardweird Croft. "Sillie" here has been taken to mean "sillak," or "sic-like," meaning "similar"—but similar to what? Similar to the Hardweird? The meaning of the word "weird" as a descriptive in both names seems to have been quite lost. I have an impression that "weird" in this sense may be akin to the Scots word "yird," sometimes spelt "yeird," or "eird," meaning "earth," and so "Hardweird" would just mean the rough, stony unpromising ground. But that is somewhat speculative, and speculation in street or place names, in Aberdeen or anywhere else, is inadmissible.*

While dealing with Hardweird, we may spare a few moments for St. John's Well, at the east end of Hardweird and Skene Row.

St. John's Well is named from the circumstance that it was situated on the piece of land known for centuries as St. John's Croft, which is believed to have been part of the property owned in Aberdeen by the Knights of St. John of Jerusalem, as the successors of the Knights Templars. The Templars had a great deal of property in the town and neighbourhood, including a chapel near the Castlegate, where St. Peter's Roman Catholic Church now stands, and, of course, a Preceptory at Maryculter.† St. John's Well

*The Hardweird Croft is well shown in the map appended to Mr. Anderson's Charters and Other Writs.

†On 22nd May, 1542, a precept of sasine was granted by Walter, Lord of St. John, Preceptor of Torphichen, in favour of the Principal and Sub-Principal of King's College, of a Templar

at Hardweird, is now, I think, the only relic that connects the city by name with this celebrated body of men. The spring long had a certain fame in the locality. We find it familiarly spoken of in 1696, in connection with the riding of the Marches, when the Baillies "keeping the high rode to Robslaw above Sant John's Well fand the north ends of the crofts" rightly observed. In the middle of the last century the well was restored by the Police Commissioners. On that occasion the existing stone-work was erected, bearing the Latin inscription written by Dr. Melvin, the noted rector of the Grammar School, which may still be read, as follows :—

SANCTI JOANNIS FONS
AB OPERUM PUBLICORUM
CURATORIBUS REFECTUS
A.D. MDCCCLII
(ST. JOHN'S WELL, RESTORED BY THE CURATORS OF
PUBLIC WORKS, 1852).

The well remained as it left the hands of the Police Commissoners in 1852 until the construction of the Rosemount Viaduct under the Act of 1883, when it was moved a few yards, and reconstructed on its present site.

The not very savoury name of Swine's Close, borne by the passage that connects Hardweird with Skene Street, has ceased to exist within the last twelve months. Those who remember this passage thirty to

Croft near the Denburn of Aberdeen—"adjacente lie Denburn in territorio occidentali croftorum burgi de Aberdene." Fasti, pp. 18, 119.

Hardweird.

Showing the Forestairs.

forty years ago will understand how it came to have its descriptive appellation, and would not be surprised that under the cleaner amenities of the present day, and as itself now very much improved, it has been made to carry the less graphic name of Skene Lane.

At the west end of Hardweird is Jack's Brae, a name that has, no doubt, puzzled a good many people. Who was Jack? It comes out in this entry in the Burgh Registers :—

> "1st April, 1758—The same day, the Council approves the feuing out of that piece of ground petitioned for by Alexander Cushnie, lying in the north side of the Denburn opposite Hardweird, betwixt the road leading to Mid Gilcomstone on the east and David Shaw's bleach eld on the west parts, as the same was propped and staiked out by the Magistrates; the west part whereof to be feued out by John Jack, manufacturer at Gilcomstone, at the yearly value of 8*s.* sterling, of yearly feu duty, and the east part thereof by the said Alexander Cushnie at the rate of 12*s.* sterling yearly, and appoints them to take out feu charters thereon accordingly."*

It was this John Jack, "manufacturer at Gilcomstone," who proceeded thereupon to feu out the west part of the ground, lying on the face of the hill, and gave the name of Jack's Brae to the street.

A friend and neighbour of John Jack of Gilcomston was Robert Mackie, skinner, who, when Jack was feuing out Jack's Brae, was also feuing out certain portions of land at the Denburnside. Among others, he feued Mackie Place, betweeen the Denburn and Skene Street, and in that street name left us a memorial of himself to our own day.

*Burgh Registers, vol. LXII., f. 203.

In these notes on street names, I have refrained, almost entirely, from dealing with obsolete names, but an exception must be made in the case of that curious name, "The Galleries," adjoining Mackie Place, which has disappeared only in recent years. I should think that name must have been a standing source of wonderment to many people. Nobody can explain it. And by the way, the wonder has not been confined to Aberdeen. "Galleries" as a place name occurs elsewhere—I find there is one in Forfarshire, but the discussion that has taken place over the meaning of the name has had no definitely satisfactory result. The most plausible explanation is that "goll," or "gall," is an obsolete Celtic vocable, meaning "a hollow," and that "Rie" means "flowing water" (compare the Ayrshire stream, the Rye)—and according to this "Gallerie" would mean the hollow of the flowing water. One would like to believe it, for it suits the Aberdeen "Galleries" so admirably.

But the "Galleries" is interesting in another way. We all know Whitehouse Street, which leads to Skene Street directly opposite the Galleries, and takes its name from the gaunt White House that still stands in what used to be the Galleries, overlooking the Denburn. Probably not very many people know, however, that in this White House once existed, not so many years ago, an actual publishing firm, whose imprint was first "The Mackie Place Company," afterwards "The Galleries Company, Skene Street." The "Company" consisted of a single family, the Forbeses, and the publications consisted of a single

Photo by Mr. Fred Hardie.

Jack's Brae.

monthly periodical, "The Castle Spectre"—named, perhaps unwittingly, after Monk Lewis's well-known play of the same name. The most curious feature about the periodical, "The Castle Spectre," which appeared regularly once a month for twelve years, was that it was wholly written (with contributions by personal friends) and printed by the family in the White House, Galleries, a private printing-press having been fitted up in the house for the purpose. Needless to say, very few copies of this strange magazine were printed off, and it is now extremely rare. If, however, anyone wishes to look at the complete volume (all that was printed) which was the copy retained by the family who printed it, they may do so in the Reference Department of the Public Library.*

On the other side of the Denburn Valley, from Mackie Place, runs Leadside Road, like so many of our streets on that side of the city, laid out on part of the Gilcomston property. The meaning of the name is clear to all who remember that the mill "lade" flowed here for many years as an open stream on its way from the Gilcomston Dam to the Gilcomston Mills at the top of Jack's Brae.†

*Of course, the actual reason for the name, "The Castle Spectre," was that the White House was said to be haunted, and it was otherwise sometimes known as the Castle. A woodcut of "The Castle" is given on the title-page of the first issue of the periodical. This and the few other woodcuts in the earlier parts were by Miss Burton, daughter of John Hill Burton, the historian.

†The Lands of Gilcomston were feued off in 12 lots, 27th July, 1765, etc. A valuable "Survey of the Lands of Gilcomston,

In following the Leadside Road we are reminded of the recent passing away of that ancient Aberdeen landmark, the Gilcomston Dam. Round it gather the associations of centuries, and as generation after generation of the young people of the town passed away it seemed as if this far from ornamental sheet of water—their playfield—were the only immutable feature of the neighbourhood. It was finally cleared away in 1908, and part of the site is already occupied by houses.* The scheme of improvement, of which the filling in of the Dam was a part, included the laying out of certain new streets at the Damside, one of which is named Craigie Park, another Whitehall Street, and the third Hope Street.† The first of these names is quite appropriate, for the new streets are laid out on the Craigie Park property. The name of Whitehall Street is also not without a certain fitness, as Whitehall Road is near, formed partly on the ground of the old Whitehall House, recently demolished. But "Hope Street" puzzles one. As the result of an inquiry on the point which I made to my friend the City Chamberlain, I was informed that

Taken by A. L. from 26th April to 10th May, 1749," is in existence, and was reproduced in the process, the Town Council *v.* the Incorporated Trades, February, 1903, with all the lots marked.

*An admirable photographic illustration of the Dam, after it had begun to be filled in, was published as a Supplement to the *Aberdeen Journal* (weekly edition), 17th November, 1909.

†The new streets were so named at a meeting of the Town Council Streets and Roads Committee, 7th January, 1909.

"Hope Street, Craigiepark, was adopted as a name by the Committee yesterday, out of a list submitted to them, as a short and euphonious name—this and nothing more."

This brings us, at length, to our last street name in this section—the Craigie Loanings, sometimes, in the old days, spelt the Craggy Loanings. A "loaning" is, of course, merely a lane; but some people may have looked about for the crags that seem to have given the name to the street. They would have some difficulty in finding them. In 1461, as the St. Nicholas Chartulary informs us, an attestation was made by the burgh of Aberdeen of certain endowments of the Altar of the Holy Cross in St. Nicholas Church. Part of these endowments was nine shillings and fourpence (Scots) from the land—meaning the tenement—of one William Beelde, in Schoolhill, between the land of Thomas Meldrum on the east, and the land of another burgess, Alexander Crag, on the west. And the attestation goes on to say:—

> "And from his (Alexander Crag's) own croft, commonly called the Cragvele lying to the west of the said burgh, near the king's highway which leads to Rubbislaw, called the Loaning . . . thirteen shillings and fourpence."*

This was Crag's Loaning, a name that in the kindly Aberdonian manner, fond of diminutives, would soon become Craggy's Loaning, and so the Craigie Loaning, a name which, having subsisted for five centuries and a half, will, we trust, be retained

*Chartulary of St. Nicholas, vol. 2, p. 49.

for many years to come. At least one attempt has ben made in our time to change the name ; perhaps it is as well that its history should be better known as something of a safeguard in the future.

CHAPTER XI

GILCOMSTON AND THE WELL OF SPA: THE "STEPS": SKENE SQUARE: MABERLY STREET AND BROADFORD: A NOTABLE ABERDEEN TRIAL: ROSEMOUNT: THE BELLEVILLE NURSERY: THE LOANINGS: LOANHEAD AND ITS QUARRIES: WALLFIELD AND BELVIDERE: THE BONNY MUIR.

ALMOST all the street names in the Rosemount district are recent, for it is a new suburb, and nearly all the street names are personal, or relate to their situation, or are purely fanciful as became so much the fashion in later years. One or two only are really historical

One of the Gilcomston group of names in this quarter is a little puzzling to the present generation, viz.—Gilcomston Steps, that part of the line of street that joins the lower part of Skene Square to Woolmanhill. We are not to suppose that, although the street here forms a slight ascent, it was ever actually a stair, like the streets of certain Continental towns that could be named. In the early part of the eighteenth century there were steps here, leading from the high ground to what was known as Nether Gilcomston. In due time, when the road—which itself is not yet two hundred years old—became a public highway, the name "The Steps of Gilcomston" continued to be applied to it.*

*In Paterson's Maps of 1746, the place is marked simply "The Steps." By the end of that century, and for a large part

The name of Skene Square, the line of street leading upward from Gilcomston Steps, is really more difficult than the "Steps" themselves. The name is not very old—not older, probably, than the later part of the eighteenth century; and the earliest actual use of it I have come across is in this public intimation of 1807:—

"For Sale—That Extensive Premises called Skene Square, which has been employed as a cart and plough work for many years, and it is well adapted for that and any other Manufactory, and the situation might be found fit for Building or Pleasure ground. For further particulars, apply to John Christie, the Proprietor." *Aberdeen Journal*, 15th April, 1807.

At that time, the name was applied only to the part of the street between the top of Maberly Street and Caroline Place, and "the premises called Skene Square" stood probably on the site of the present Skene Square School. Sometimes it was known as Skene's Square, but there was no special significance in that. My own impression is that the name of Skene was applied simply because, like the other streets leading westward, Skene Street, and the Skene Road, it was on a line of road that led towards Skene.*

of last century "The Steps of Gilcomston" is the name. In 1852, it has become simply "Gilcomstom Steps." It has always been rather a poor neighbourhood, long inhabited by weavers.

*What seems to have been the very first property in Skene Square is referred to in the following Minute of the Town Council—27th September, 1665.—"The Council agrees to a request by Walter Melvill, tacksman of the Loch, that as "he

White House, Galleries.

Gives the name to Whitehouse Street.

The name of Maberly Street, in which the Broadford Works stand, continues the name of John Maberly, an early proprietor of the works, and a man of more than local note. He was M.P. for Abington, Berkshire, and at one time he thought of a close connection with Aberdeen in this regard, but he was not encouraged in that by the Aberdeen Magistrates. He was presented with the freedom of the town, however, in 1818, by the Town Council, "as a mark of their respect and the high sense they entertain of his spirited exertions in introducing several branches of useful manufacture in this city and neighbourhood, which have not failed to produce increased industry and prosperity among the manufacturing classes of the community."*

Not long after this, in 1820, took place what was long remembered as the most exciting legal case for many years in Aberdeen—the action of James Skene of Rubislaw, Walter Scott's friend, against John and Stephen Maberly and their partners of Broadford Works, relative to the pollution of the Rubislaw Burn by their new Bleachfield. The ablest lawyers from the Edinburgh bar were there, Henry Cockburn for

had bein at vast charges and expenssis in drying and wineing (winning? reclaiming) of the said Loch," he is granted the liberty of a piece of waste ground "at the west part of the said Loch, neir to the commone hieway going from the toune to the Burk Mill, near the lands of Dub Castell," for the use of a dwelling house, barn, and barnyard. Council Registers (Burgh Rec. Soc.), II., 222-3.

**Aberdeen Journal*, 25th November, 1818.

Skene, and Francis Jeffrey for the Maberlys, who ultimately won their cause, and their bleachfield was carried on at Rubislaw till within the last year or two, when the pressure of an extending city caused its removal to the more distant neighbourhood of the Bridge of Dee.*

The failure of the Maberly Bank and other commercial undertakings of the family occurred in 1832. By that time John Maberly had ceased to have any connection with Broadford works, but the street name recalls the period of his greatest vogue in the north of Scotland, as well as the early days of this still prosperous local undertaking.

The name of Spa Street presents no difficulty. It is taken from the Well of Spa, situated in this street, so long noted for its medicinal properties It is in many ways the most interesting of the wells of Aberdeen.† For many years the open Gilcomston Burn ran along Spa Street, but in 1848 the Police Commissioners had it covered over in pursuance of a consistently followed policy for the improvement of the streets of the town. Up till 1889 the part of the street from Skene Street to what is now Gilcomston Park was known as Well of Spa, but in that year this name was abolished as a street name, and Spa Street

*The last of the Rubislaw bleachfield was the felling of the great chimney stalk which took place on the evening of 17th July, 1908, in view of many thousands of the townspeople.

†The story of the Well of Spa is set out in Historical Aberdeen, pp. 136, *et seq.*

was made to apply to the whole length of street from Skene Street to Skene Square.*

The part of the lands of Gilcomston on which Baker Street was afterwards laid out, was bought in 1867 by the Baker Incorporation, hence the name of the street. The same body laid out, within the last quarter of a century, the adjoining Raeburn Place, on the same property, and named it after the Deacon of the craft, Peter Raeburn, baker, Schoolhill. Stevenson Street, which lies at such a curiously inconvenient level at the opposite side of Rosemount Viaduct from Baker Street, bears the name of its first proprietor, W. S. Stevenson, tea merchant, Belmont Street, well known at one time as a volunteer officer in the city.† The Street was laid out some years before the construction of the Viaduct, and promised to become useful as a direct connecting street between the Denburn district and Rosemount. But the great scheme of the Schoolhill and Rosemount Viaduct, carried out under the Extension Act of 1883, destroyed at once the appearance of the street and its use.

The curiously named street, Farmers' Hall Lane, is much more modern than its name would suggest. There were no houses there until well into last century, and the name was not in use, so far as I can make out, till the sixties. It appears in the Aberdeen Directory for the first time in 1867-68. The name seems to

*See Minutes of Town Council, 17th June, 1889.

†He took out the ground for the building of the Imperial Hotel, and otherwise entered considerably into prospective building schemes. He resided at Viewfield.

have arisen from the circumstance that part of the property in the lane—now used as dwelling houses—was used for many years as a granary, where farmers met to do business. The granary was carried on by William Anderson, grain merchant, at one time o Barkmill, afterwards of Maybank House, Hutcheon Street, where he died about 1865. There are persons still alive in Aberdeen who remember Anderson's granary well, and the beginnings of Farmers' Hall Lane as a street name.

Mount Street and South Mount Street are named from their situation on the upper slopes of the elevated ground now generally known as Rosemount. This name comes in the first instance, so far as I can make out, from the residential property so named, which lay on the north side of what was for long known as the Stocket Road, and is now Rosemount Place, the main road running along the ridge of the district westwards. Rosemount is a purely fanciful name, not older, probably, than the beginning of last century. Rosemount House stood within its grounds, on the north side of Rosemount Place, a little west of Forbes Street. It stands there still, in reduced circumstances, obscured by a curtain of new tenement houses and shops that have been built recently between it and the street. Apart from its being the centre and origin of the district name, Rosemount House has little of historical interest. This notice must date from about its beginning:

"Rosemount. To be Let. The House, Garden, and Offices called Rosemount, situated a little to the west of

Skene's Square, at present occupied by Mrs. Mitchell. Apply to David Hutcheon, advocate."*

By the middle of last century, Rosemount House was the property and residence of Baillie John Urquhart, and still later, of Robert Stevens, grocer, a Town Councillor and a well-known business man in his day.

Rosemount Terrace was the first street to carry the district name. It was laid out in 1829. Mount Street was laid out on the same property, and dates from 1847. Here is the public intimation of the formation of the new street:

"Building Areas. Rosemount. A New Street having been formed through the Lands of Rosemount, leading from the Old Skene Road towards the Mid Stocket Road, opposite the Lunatic Asylum, Building Areas will now be feued along the street. They measure 240 feet in depth. The situation is airy, and there is a delightful view of the surrounding country. The Water and Gas have been conveyed to the end of the street; but the street is without the bounds of the Police, and there are *no Police Rates nor Public Burdens payable for the ground.* Apply to Mr. F. Edmond, advocate, 64 Union Street."†

South Mount Street, formed some years afterwards, was laid out partly on what was known as Belleville Nursery, which stretched away westwards as far as Jack's Brae and Short Loanings. Prior to the laying

**Aberdeen Journal*, 10th January, 1827.

†*Aberdeen Journal*, 27th January, 1847, repeated in *Aberdeen Herald*, 11th September, 1847. The first house erected was the cottage, still standing, in the triangular piece of ground at the foot of the street.

out of South Mount Street, the nurseryman was James Reid, Jr., of the family of James Reid & Co., afterwards Ben. Reid & Co., well-known as nurserymen throughout a great part of last century. James Reid's residence was the villa of Belleville, Gilcomston, afterwards used as the Incurable Hospital.*

From Rosemount Place, the main central thoroughfare of the district, Short Loanings carries us to Leadside Road. The Short Loaning is a descriptive name used to distinguish the street from the Craigie Loaning in the same neighbourhood. Loaning, of course, is simply a country lane, and the "s" in the names of Short Loanings and Craigie Loanings is a meaningless addition which ought to be dropped.

People have wondered sometimes, no doubt, at the name of Magdala Place, the short street which abuts on Short Loanings about half-way down that thoroughfare. About the middle of the seventies the street was formed and the houses put up there by the late Henry Brechin Pirie—a connection of the once well-known Councillor Henry Brechin. Mr. Pirie was much interested at the time in the expedition to Abyssinia and the capture of Magdala, the capital, and carried his interest into the name of his new street. The Town Council formally sanctioned the name on the transference of the property to the present owner in 1892.

The most interesting street name in this locality is Loanhead Terrace, but as it happens, the name is

*Another James Reid was at the same time a nurseryman at Springbank Nursery, Ferryhill, where Springbank Terrace now is.

topographically in the wrong place. The hamlet of Loanhead was situated near what is now Mile End corner, at the top of Craigie Loanings (which is the "Loan" in question). The houses were mostly occupied by those employed at the Loanhead Quarries, first opened there about 1730 by James Emslie, an enterprising person, who may be said to be the father of the granite quarrying industry of Aberdeen.* In 1780, a visitor to Rubislaw says of Loanhead:

> "Turning to the north-east, we rode up to a village called Loanhead, from which there is a fine prospect of the town, the harbour, the sea, Old Aberdeen, and the adjacent country. From the Bridge of Dee to the river mouth, the country seems one continuous village. This place was formerly wholly possessed by labourers who wrought in the adjacent quarries, or was the occasional residence of beggars, who were not permitted to settle in town. There are now many decent houses in it, and the fields around are in high culture."†

Loanhead Terrace is a considerable distance east of where Loanhead hamlet stood, but fortunately it perpetuates the name and the associations. The street was laid out half-a-century ago by the Wrights and Coopers' Incorporation, still the superiors of the ground.

The adjoining Watson Street is on ground feued out by the Shoemaker Incorporation, about the time Loanhead Terrace came into being, on ground formerly

*I believe the central block of Gordon's College Buildings, erected by Adam, 1740, is built of Loanhead granite.

†Francis Douglas' Description of the East Coast, 1782, p. 131.

known as Drywell Park. It was named after Baillie George Watson, shoemaker, Deacon of the Craft at that time.* Thomson Street was also laid by the Incorporated Trades. It was named after Mr. James Thomson, then of Messrs Buyers & Co., house carpenters, Kidd Lane, now (1910) a valuator in the city. Mr. Thomson filled the office of Factor of the Widows' Funds of the Craft.

The Wallfield streets—Wallfield Place and Wallfield Crescent—were laid out only a few years ago on the grounds of Wallfield House. It has been suggested that the name is properly Well-field (Sc. Wall), but I have never found any evidence of this. Moreover, it is not an old name. In 1826 a notice appeared in the newspapers intimating that "the Property of Wallfield, formerly called Lower Belvidere, on the Stocket Road" was to sell or let,† which would seem to show that the name was then quite recent.

The Belvidere group of streets in this quarter are from the fanciful name applied to the house occupied in the beginning of last century by John Ewing of Shelagreen. Such names as applied to residential properties in this neighbourhood were rather common in the early years of last century. Thus, we had

*Baillie Watson's portrait, by Stirling, is among the portraits in Trinity Hall. Alexander Watson, 1744-1831, author of "The Kail Brose of Auld Scotland," and the still better known "Wee Wifikie," was also a Deacon of the Aberdeen Incorporated Trades. He was a "merchant tailor."

†*Aberdeen Journal*, 12th April, 1826.

The Hardgate.

From a painting by Mr. Alec C. Fraser, belonging to Mr. David Gray.

Westfield, on one side of the Craigie Loanings, and on the other Craigie Park, the property of John Ross, the noted organist of St. Paul's Episcopal Chapel. Not far off was Westburn, which became the property of Chalmers, of the *Aberdeen Journal*, in the middle of last century, although the name had already been in use for half-a-century before. The present Westburn House, now within the Westburn Park, built by Chalmers in 1845, was one of the later works of Archibald Simpson, architect.*

A few of the street names in the Mile End quarter call for passing notice. Mile End itself is an importation like Adelphi, Long Acre, etc. Hosefield Avenue, Cairnfield Place, and Bonnymuir Place are all laid out on ground owned by the University of Aberdeen, and all rightly perpetuate the names of old lands upon which they are constructed. It was at the request of the University Authorities that the Town Council agreed to apply these names to the new streets—Bonnymuir Place, Mile End Avenue, and Cairnfield Place, in January, 1890, and Hosefield Avenue in 1893. On the Bonny Moor, as it was called in the eighteenth century, there used to be one of the noted wells of the district, but all trace of it has long ago disappeared.

*The stream now known as the Westburn was formerly known as the Clerkseat Burn.

CHAPTER XII

CARDEN PLACE: SKENE OF RUBISLAW AND WEST END STREET NAMES: JAMES GILES, ARTIST, AND RUBISLAW TERRACE: THE LAND ASSOCIATION AND ITS WORK: ST. SWITHIN STREET: FOUNTAINHALL ROAD: THE STOCKET FOREST AND RUBISLAW NEIGHBOURHOOD: CONCLUSION.

THE streets in the west end of the city are mostly recent, and not many of the street names have associations of far past persons or events. And yet, certain of these names are not to be overlooked.

Carden Place, part of the main road leading towards Skene, and now filled with villa residences, recalls a historical personage of international celebrity. In 1552, when Jerome Cardan, the noted physician, mathematician, and astrologer of Pavia, was on a visit to Scotland, treating Archbishop Hamilton of St. Andrews for an asthmatic affection, he visited Aberdeen University, the then comparatively new northern seat of learning. While in Aberdeen, he had his attention drawn to the water supply of the town, obtained at that time mainly from certain well known spring wells. One of these wells, noted for many years, was situated in the suburban hollow near the Denburn, and from the association with the noted visitor it was ever afterwards known as Carden's Well. There is some suggestion that other wells in town were spoken of in the same way, but this is the only one that retained the name till our day.* Indeed, as early as 1708 the name was applied strictly to this particular well, for we read that in connection with the bringing of the first water supply properly so-called to the town in that year, the Council made an agreement with masons "for building the first font (or cistern) at the spring of Cardanus Well for ten pound sterling."† Carden's Well gave the name many years ago to the hollow or haugh in which it was situated, and when the new line of houses began to be built on the ground the street naturally received the name of Carden Place. And so the name of the famous philosopher is perpetuated in the north of Scotland.‡

Carden Terrace, part of the same line of street, is very recent, and takes its name from the same source. The short line of houses forming the Terrace were erected by the late Mr. James Henderson, arctitect, in 1867, and the name was first applied at that time.

*Mr. P. J. Anderson recently described a most interesting and rare pamphlet, now in the Bodleian Library, Oxford, that relates to Cardan's visit to Aberdeen, embodying certain poetical descriptions of Aberdeen Wells. It is of date 1707 (no place or printer's name). See *Scottish Notes and Queries*, December, 1906.

†Burgh Registers (Record Society Publications) II., pp. 333-4.

‡Unfortunately, the only existing "Life" of Cardan in volume form—Jerome Cardan: By W. G. Waters, 1898—omits all mention of his visit to Aberdeen.

The line of street which runs from the top of Union Street westward, and joins Carden Place at Queen's Cross, has the name of Alford Place for part of its length, and Albyn Place for the rest.

While still a rough country road, Alford Place was known simply as the Alford Road, being the direct line of highway—the coach road, indeed—from Aberdeen to Alford and Upper Donside. Albyn Place, as both a street and a street name, came much later, about 1830, when Archibald Simpson, architect, was engaged erecting his villa residences there. The name was borrowed, I think, from the Albyn Place of Edinburgh, one of the fashionable streets of the new town. James Skene of Rubislaw, proprietor of most of the ground on which Albyn Place of Aberdeen was laid out, lived in the new town of Edinburgh, a close friend and neighbour of Sir Walter Scott, and we can easily see the association that resulted in the transference of the street name to Aberdeen.

It is due to James Skene of Rubislaw that we have that handsome line of houses along the north side of Albyn Place, separated from it by the line of gardens, which carries the name of Rubislaw Terrace. The scheme of streets, of which this formed a part, was the design originally of Archibald Simpson—along with Rubislaw Place, Waverley Place, and other new streets of the quarter. And here, again, we have a trace of the Walter Scott connection. This was in the early thirties of last century. Some of the minor streets of the scheme were opened then, but it was not till 1852 that Rubislaw Terrace, the most imposing and expensive street of the quarter, was actually brought into being. Archibald Simpson had passed away by that time, and the street as we know it is on a different design from his.

Says an Aberdeen newspaper of the time:

"We understand that plans have been sketched for a new terrace of houses proposed to be erected on the property of Mr. Skene of Rubislaw, on the north side of Albyn Place. The style of architecture possesses in a high degree the rare merit of combining what is new, at least in Aberdeen, with what is, in point of taste, exceedingly beautiful. It does not admit of a more precise designation, but may be described as in the style of the renowned Abbotsford House—a combination of the Scottish and Elizabethan orders. The houses alternate in pairs: the one of a superior description, having handsome bow windows, reaching the height of both floors, with a neat balustrade; the other with plain windows. In each case the door is reached by a flight of steps—an arrangement attained by the basement floor being half-sunk. The interior arrangements would be exceedingly commodius, and possessed of every requisite that even luxury itself could suggest. The dining-rooms in the case of the superior character of houses would, by means of the bow window, be 30 feet in length, and the other 25 feet. The extent of the terrace, as planned, would be about 1,500 feet, with a depth of feu of about 150. This is exclusive of pleasure grounds in front, between which and the houses there will, we believe, be a road or drive, with approaches. The plan, which embraces about fifty houses, is the joint production of Mr. Giles, artist, and Messrs. MacKenzie & Matthews, architects. It is truly a splendid project (the merits of which cannot be sufficiently unfolded in a written description), and by the enterprize of Mr. Skene, the proprietor, backed by public-spirited citizens taking feus, its realisation would seem to be attainable. The situation is one of the best about the city." *

When we reach Queen's Cross we enter on the neighbourhood that has had its appearance completely transformed in recent times by the operations of the Aberdeen Land Association. The pioneer work of this Association in what would now be termed town planning, in the outlying parts of Aberdeen, has been the making of the external districts of the city during the last thirty years. And when we remember that the Association has been carried on entirely as a private business undertaking, we can appreciate the enterprise and public spirit of its promoters and advisers.

The Land Association was incorporated in March, 1875, with the object of purchasing land in the vicinity of Aberdeen on a large scale, and feuing—or re-selling it in smaller lots. At the very outset the Association acquired the properties of Rubislaw (so long the heritage of the Skene family), Fountainhall, and Morningfield, in the western suburbs of the city, and Torry and Craiginches on the south side of the Dee, for the aggregate price of £134,000. It was on these properties that so many of the newer streets of Aberdeen have been laid out that have added so much to the beauty and convenience of the city.†

**Aberdeen Journal.* Quoted in *Aberdeen Herald*, 3rd April, 1852.

†The first directors of the Land Association were Thomas Adam, banker, Sir Alex. Anderson, Robert Catto of Wallfield,

St. Swithin Street, near Queen's Cross, on the property acquired by the Land Association, was laid out before the formation of the Association—that is, in 1869—by the late Dr. Francis Edmund, who held Rubislaw as trustee on the sequestrated estate of Sir Alexander Anderson. Dr. Edmund bestowed the name, having a humourous appreciation of the quaint versified "Legend of St. Swithin," as written by the late George Davidson, and illustrated by Faed.* In the earlier years this street was named South St. Swithin Street, the intention being to apply the name North St. Swithin Street to the other half of the street on the north side of Queen's Cross, begun in 1876, and now named Fountainhall Road. This street was, in fact, named North St. Swithin Street for some years after it was made, but that was felt to be a clumsy expedient, and accordingly the change was effected in favour of the present name.

John G. Chalmers, James Crombie of Grandholm, Alex. Davidson of Desswood, Alex. Edmund, Jr. of Kingswells, Robert Lumsden, banker, John Reid, advocate, Jas. Augustus Sinclair (afterwards Earl of Caithness), Robert Urquhart, merchant, and James Walker, 52 Union Street. The first Chairman was Robert Urquhart (after whom Urquhart Road is named), who held that office till his death in 1877. For much interesting information relative to the Land Association and its work, I am indebted to the courtesy of Mr. Alex. Ledingham, S.S.C., Secretary of the Association.

*George Davidson, long known as a bookseller in Aberdeen, died at Loris Bank, Cults, 10th May, 1872. There were two editions of "St. Swithin"—1st edition, 1856, 2nd edition, illustrated by Faed, 1861—reprinted, 1864. His other works are now forgotten.

Stanley Street, which touches St. Swithin Street, was laid out in 1876. Feuing was begun in the street by the late Mr. William Keith, of Rubislaw Den House, one of the promoters of the Land Association. He was the father-in-law of Mr. H. O. Forbes, famous as an explorer in New Guinea, and having a warm interest in all adventures of an exploring kind, and a keen admiration of the late Henry M. Stanley, he got the new street named after him, Stanley Street.*

Fountainhall Road perpetuates the name of one of the quaint old properties of the district, although, as I imagine, in a corrupt form. The small property which Fountainhall House came to be built upon was originally part of the lands of Gilcomston, within a stone-throw of the Gilcomston Dam. In 1753 this lot of the Gilcomston lands was feud to Alexander Dyce, merchant in Aberdeen, who thereupon, it is concluded, although definite proof has never been found, erected the house, which came to be known as Fountainhall House. We do not actually find the name Fountainhall, however, until we reach 1783, after which it runs through the writs till the present time.† But the ground there contained some of the old stone fountains, or cisterns, used from 1706 as storage wells for the Aberdeen water supply, and on

*An amusing story is told of how Mr. Keith, not being certain of carrying the directors of the Association with him in this matter, had the name of the street painted up during the night. It was allowed to remain.

†The first actual mention of Fountainhall that I have found is in Taylor's map of 1773.

Union Street.

From Windmill Brae and Crown Terrace, *c.* 1828-30.

this account the neighbourhood was spoken of as Fountainha'. This, however, is not "Fountainhall," but Fountain-haugh, or hollow, and in naming the property Fountainhall, Dyce or his successor, Professor Copland, who occupied Fountainhall House till his death in 1822, either consciously for euphony, or unconsciously from ignorance, perpetrated the name Fountainhall House, still borne by the old residence, and also as a street name by Fountainhall Road.*

Beyond Queen's Cross, we find the name Queen's Gate applied to the quadrangle formed by the junction of Queen's Road and Forest Road. This may suggest the old style designation of Queen's Gait, for "the King's high-gait," meaning the King's Highway, was a usual designation in the old days. But that interesting meaning does not apply here. It is merely a fanciful name, suggested by the two principal feuars of the ground, and adopted by the authorities. The name of King's Gate was applied to the corresponding spot at the junction of the north end of Forest Road and South Stocket Road, but as the last named street was gradually feued off, the name King's Gate came to be applied to the whole new line of houses between Forest Road and Fountainhall Road.

*Those interested in the detail story of Fountainhall House will find much delightful matter in the small volume "Vanishing Aberdeen, Fountainhall House," etc., by the late Dr. Cruickshank, 1894. It is not too much to say that this is one of the best little monographs on local topographical history that Aberdeen has produced.

Stocket Road is the most interesting street name in the neighbourhood. There are three of them—the Low Stocket, the Mid Stocket, and the South Stocket Roads. They run over the ground covered by, and perpetuate the name of, the old Stocket Forest, one of the seven royal hunting forests of Aberdeenshire.* It is a name intimately associated with the liberties of Aberdeen. The Stocket Forest was granted to the Aberdonians in 1313 by Robert the Bruce, for signal services rendered; but in 1494 James IV., in some capricious mood, granted it to Sir Andrew Wood, which was so passionately resented by the citizens that they carried the matter before the Privy Council, and this iniquitous grant, which would probably have had the effect of reducing Aberdeen to a mere burgh of barony, was annulled.†

It was in the Stocket Forest that the incident occurred—or is said to have occurred—in the saving of the King from a ferocious wolf, which was slain by a Highland follower with his skein or dagger. His reward was a grant of land in the forest, and thus arose the family of Skene, and the property of Skene, which continues to be a place name on the lands in our own day.‡

*The other six royal hunting forests were Mar, Birse, Drum-oak, Benachie, Kintore and Dyce.

†The whole episode, so creditable to the independence or spirit of the burghers, is dealt with in Historical Aberdeen, pp. 18-21.

‡In those days wolves were common enough in the neighbourhood. In 1457 an Act of James II., ordained "for the

It is a curious thing that the very earliest entries in our Aberdeen Burgh Register deal with the Stocket Forest. That invaluable series of registers run continuously (with the exception of a single volume) from 1398 to the present time. On 18th November, 1398, we are told, "Mathew Pynches placed himself under the will of the court for having neglected to discharge (the duties of) the office of Forester, which he ought to have done."*

Then in the same year, 1398, "David Walker, Alexander Bennerman, Mathew Pinks, and William Spelding, Keepers of the Forest, were fined eight pennies for destroying, or suffering others to destroy, Deers."†

Through centuries the Stocket Forest had suffered, but part of it, at least, was still under wood at the beginning of the eighteenth century, for the Magistrates of Aberdeen, "anxious to deprive marauders of the shelter afforded them by the Forest of the Stocket, gave permission to such of the citizens as chose to take wood from it for that purpose to add balconies to the fronts of their houses, projecting eight or ten feet into the street, viz.—to the extent occupied by the outer stairs."‡

destruction of wolves," that the magistrates "sall gader the countrie folk three tymis in the yere betwix Saint Merks Day and Lammes for that is the tyme of the quhelpis." Acts of the Parls. of Scot. II., p. 51-2.

*The first entry (rendered) in Extracts from the Aberdeen Burgh Registers, I., p. 3.

†Ross's Antiquities of Aberdeen, p. 6.

‡New Statistical Account, XII., pp. 22-3.

In a very few years after this a wiser counsel was at work for preserving or re-planting the Stocket with trees. The example of Skene of Rubislaw had an influence, as will be seen from the following:—

> "9th May, 1747—It having been overtured [to the Town Council] that the Stocket Forest would be greatly beautified if the same was planted, and that it would be beneficial to the Treasury in the process of time, the Magistrates and Council foresaid agreed to visit the said Forest, and consider of the said overture."*

Two months later, the Magistrates and Council duly paid a visit to the ground—the neighbourhood about where Rubislaw Quarries now lie. And we have this statement of the result of their inspection:

> 23rd July, 1747—The Magistrates and Council, in view "that for many yers there has been a view and design of inclosing and planting the part of the Stocket which is in the sight of the town, as also a piece to the westward of the Cairn of Stocket"—a scheme hitherto delayed through the multiplicity of the town's business—"agreed that the same ought instantly to be inclosed and afterwards planted with firrs and birtch, which will not only greatly beautify that prospect from the town, but in the course of time will become very beneficial to the treasury, as is evident from Robslaw's planting in that neighbourhood."†

Forest Road, one of the newer streets in this quarter, relates also to the Stocket, and is also laid out on the Stocket ground. Forest Avenue, which is a continuation of Forest Road, south of the Skene

*Council Register, LXI., p. 284.

†Council Register LXI., pp. 235 *et seq.* It was resolved also that a Forester should be appointed, who should stay on the Stocket ground, and oversee the work. I doubt if these excellent afforestation designs came to very much.

Road, was originally named South Forest Road, but, as in the case of the two St. Swithin Streets, it was felt to be a clumsy arrangement, and so it was departed from. This name of Forest Road, it is interesting to recall, was suggested for that whole line of street by Sir Alexander Anderson, Lord Provost of the City, who wished the historic associations of the old Stocket Forest to be thus preserved.

Sir Alexander Anderson has the credit of naming another of the fine new streets there, viz.—Hamilton Place. He did so, after Dr. Hamilton, Professor of Mathematics in Marischal College, a neighbour and close personal friend of Professor Copland, of Fountainhall House. Professor Hamilton, who was a son of Gavin Hamilton, the well-known bookseller and publisher of Edinburgh, well deserved that his name should be remembered in Aberdeen. He was intensely interested in everything connected with the public advantage of the city. In 1792, he and his friend Professor Copland examined and reported on the water supply of the town, and had their services acknowledged by the Town Council appropriately in their being admitted free burgesses of the city without the payment of the usual composition.*

*Council Register, LXVI., pp. 195, 200, 211, etc. Professor Hamilton died 14th July, 1829. A public movement took place to provide a suitable memorial of this public spirited citizen, which resulted in the tall classic monument on his grave in St. Nicholas Churchyard, near the facade. His life is sketched by Ramsay in his selected writings, and was written for the Encyclopaedia Britannica (7th edn.) by Thomson of Banchory.

The other street names in the Fountainhall and Rubislaw quarter have not very much significance. Beaconsfield Place, on the north side of Queen's Road, was intended to balance Gladstone Place on the south. Hartington Road is of the same group, and it is curiously in keeping with actual things that the last stage of this eminently respectable west-end street carries the title of Devonshire Road. Desswood Place was named after Mr. Alexander Davidson of Desswood, who was chairman for several years of the Land Association, on whose property the street is laid out. Another chairman of the Association was the late Professor Dove Wilson, who fulfilled otherwise many offices in the public life of Aberdeen. His fellow-directors in the Association wished to pay him a compliment in giving his name to a street, but he preferred that the honour should be associated with the name of his deceased wife, one of the Carnegies of Redhall. And so we have Carnegie Crescent, a fine street in the higher part of the district, which has no houses built on it as yet, but will in due time be one of the finest crescents in the west end of the City.

The name of Cromwell Road, in this neighbourhood, might naturally set people wondering. The street is really a continuation of the long line of Union Grove, but for various reasons it was considered inadvisable, when the street was formed in 1903, to continue the name of Union Grove further west. Strathcona Road was the name first suggested by the feuars to the Town Council, as a distinguished name, and in honour of Lord Strathcona, who had gone from Aberdeen to do empire work in the far west. The Town Council Committee, for the sake of consistency, and discounting imagination, suggested plain Union Grove. But a personal name of distinction was desired by the feuars. Acute politicians were ruled out, for it had been found already, in the case of Gladstone Place and Beaconsfield Place, which were laid out simultaneously, that Conservatives would not take feus in the one, nor Liberals in the other. Accordingly, Oliver Cromwell was selected as a safe personality, meeting all requirements, and ultimately the Town Council accepted Cromwell Road as the designation of the street.

In passing from Carnegie Crescent we pass from the bounds of the city proper into Angusfield, the new suburban district, where the streets are just beginning to be formed. It reminds us of Alexander Angus, the noted bookseller of the Narrow Wynd, who bought the land in the middle of the eighteenth century, and not only gave his name to it, but reclaimed it from the moorland that then encircled the city on the landward side. His work in clearing the land of boulder stones may be gauged from the eight-foot "consumption dyke," constructed of these boulders, which still forms part of the garden wall of Angusfield Farm.

Perhaps I ought to apologise to readers for the length to which these notes on our street names have run. Let it be remembered, however, that they might so easily have been much longer, for nearly all obsolete names have been left out, as well as most of the names of Lanes and Courts, and nearly all fanciful and high-sounding names, mostly recent, and of no historical value. It will be entirely the fault of these chapters if what has been said does not bring home to all who love the city, and are interested in its history and traditions, that even in our street names we have a certain heritage which we ought carefully to guard. There is character, as well as history, in our street names. They reveal to us a succession of sober-minded, earnest people, not given to pretence or display, or seeking distinction much, whose quiet courage and patience are still, and by nature must be for many years to come, foundation qualities of our Scottish character. How can we best preserve the knowledge and inspiration of these things for our successors? The town of Brechin once enacted, with something of a heroic spirit, that the ancient, as well as the new names of its streets should be painted up to keep them in the public memory. Such an arrangement would have obvious inconveniences. But one feels that something should be done, in our schools especially, so that our children should not grow up in ignorance of the many things that lie about them on every hand in this town which may so easily be known, and are so well worthy of being remembered.

Supplement

SINCE 1911 the City boundary has been extended three times, gathering in on each occasion territories and communities with their own interesting histories and personal associations. The most fundamental change was brought about in 1975 when the Local Government (Scotland) Act created a new City District, embracing a number of large villages where the residents continue to be immensely proud of their individual associations with the past, and where in fact street names sometimes duplicate those in the former City.

Until 1975 the responsibility for the naming of streets rested with the Town Council, acting usually on reports submitted by the City Engineer to the Streets and Works Committee. Ward Representatives were invited to make recommendations, based on their knowledge of the historical, territorial and personal associations of their areas, and on many occasions advice was sought from local historians such as Fenton Wyness, A.A. Cormack, Marcus Milne or Cuthbert Graham. County Councillors were similarly involved in street naming, and to them we owe the preservation of names of territories, estates and farms in the former suburban areas.

At the present time the City District Authority is responsible for the naming of all streets within its bounds. Suggestions are often received from developers, but all proposed names are remitted for consideration to the Lord

Provost and the Ward Representative. Finally, opinions are sought from the Head Postmaster and the Emergency Services, for confusion with existing names could have serious consequences.

Many of our streets are named from local estates, farms and mansion-houses, while others perpetuate ancient territorial names which otherwise may be found only on old charters or maps. Natural features such as hills, burns or marshes are a popular choice, as are cairns, wells and other man-made structures. Important events in the City's history are also commemorated and we find streets named from the families or individuals who participated. Some personal names are included because their owners feued a particular piece of land, while others have been chosen to honour achievements in art, letters, science or missionary work. The influence of the early Church is evident also for there are streets named after saints, bishops, churches and church lands.

Aberdeen's special connection with Royalty has not been forgotten and we have street names which recall the visits and favours of the early Scottish Kings, while others demonstrate the City's loyalty to monarchs of a later age. The Provosts "Boord" has also provided many worthy names and from time to time Councillors or officials have been similarly honoured for outstanding services. To the social historian, however, some of the most interesting street names must be those with an industrial connection, for these commemorate the entrepreneurs of the past and the mills which were once the life-blood of some of our local communities.

Derivations are not exclusively local, for national events

have also made their mark on the City and her people. Victorian statesmen were honoured on several occasions, and in 1946 the names of leaders of the Allied Forces were chosen as a reminder of their contribution to our survival.

In recent years, Aberdeen's position as the commercial and cultural centre of the North-East has been emphasised by the naming of streets after villages, lochs and woodlands in Aberdeenshire and beyond, while well-established links with the Northern Isles have been demonstrated in the use of island names from both Orkney and Shetland.

Some examples from the period up to 1980 are as follows:-

ABBOTS PLACE

Early in the 13th century the Lands of Nigg were granted by Alexander II to the Abbey of Arbroath. Successive Abbots of Arbroath were "Barons" of Torry, which enjoyed the privileges of a Burgh of Barony until the Reformation.

ABBOTSWELL CRESCENT/DRIVE/ROAD

The "Abbots Walls" were the boundary walls of the lands which belonged to the Abbey of Arbroath. The farm and house of Abbotswells were later part of the Estate of Kincorth.

ABOYNE GARDENS/PLACE/ROAD

James Gordon, Viscount Aboyne and son of the Marquess of Huntly, was commander of the King's forces at the Battle of the Bridge of Dee on 19th June 1639. He was defeated by Montrose but later served under him when the latter embraced the royalist cause. Aboyne defected before the Battle of Philiphaugh and was excommunicated by the General Assembly in 1644.

ALEXANDER DRIVE/TERRACE

Field Marshal Harold R.L.G. Alexander, 1st. Earl Alexander of Tunis (1891–1969). He commanded the First Division of the B.E.F. in France and was in charge of the Dunkirk evacuation. As Commander-in-Chief of Allied Forces in the Middle-East, he co-ordinated the capture of Tunisia. In 1944/5 he was Supreme Allied Commander in the Mediterranean. He served as Governor-General of Canada from 1946–1952.

ANDERSON AVENUE

Sir John Anderson (1814–1886). A native of Woodside, he gained fame as a designer of machinery and armaments for the War Department, and was knighted by Queen Victoria in 1878. He gifted the Anderson Library to the people of Woodside, establishing a Trust for its maintenance and for prizes at Woodside School.

ANDERSON DRIVE

Sir Alexander Anderson (1802–1887). An advocate in Aberdeen, he was associated with numerous undertakings of public benefit including the Aberdeen Dispensary, the Aberdeen Market Company and the Great North of Scotland Railway. He entered the Town Council in 1859 and was immediately elected Lord Provost. He held office till 1866 and among the improvements which he organised were the water supply from the Dee at Cairnton, the new Municipal and County Buildings and the construction of several new streets. He was also the originator of Aberdeen Land Association and one of its first Directors.

ARBROATH LANE/PLACE/WAY

The Abbey of Arbroath or Aberbrothoc was founded by William the Lion in 1178 in memory of Thomas Becket, the murdered Archbishop of Canterbury. He endowed it with extensive lands and amongst its possessions were the Lands of Nigg, which included the whole of the present-day Torry and Kincorth.

ARNAGE CRESCENT/DRIVE/ETC.

Provost John Ross of Arnage and Clochan (1665–1714). A wealthy merchant, he is associated with the Lands of Mastrick which at one time belonged to the Ross family.

ASHLEY GARDENS/PARK/ETC.

Originally part of the Lands of Rubislaw, the estate of Ashley was first named Friendship Farm. The name was changed to Ashley in the late 19th century, supposedly because of the number of ash trees there. It was acquired by John Cook, shipowner, in 1857.

ASHTOWN PLACE/WALK

There were at one time two farms in Newhills Parish named Ashiehillock and Esseyhillock, later united under the name of Ashtown. Esseyhillock is said to mean "Hillock of the ash trees", but "essie" can also mean "ashy" or "cindery".

AUCHINLECK ROAD

Field-Marshal Sir Claude John Eyre Auchinleck (1884–1981). He was Commander-in-Chief in India in January 1941 and from 1941–1942 he commanded the British Forces in the Middle-East. He withdrew past Tobruk but inflicted a decisive defeat on the Axis at El Alamein. In 1943 he resumed his post as C. in C. India.

AUCHINYELL GARDENS/ROAD/TERRACE

This was the name of a small property which stood near the bridge, built to carry the road over the Deeside Railway. The name is said to mean "Field of the fold" from "Achadh" (field) and "chuith" (fold).

AUCHMILL ROAD

The estate of Auchmull or Auchmollen was part of the Barony of Grandhome. Auchmill House was built about 1750 and was famed for its deer park. The name means "bald or bare field".

AUCHRINY CIRCLE

This was an old territorial name for Stoneywood and it is mentioned in 1367 as being made up of two parts known as the Waterton and the Welton.

AULDEARN GARDENS/PLACE/ROAD

The Battle of Auldearn was fought on 9th May 1645. Montrose's Royalist forces gained a great victory over the Covenanters commanded by Major-General Hurry. Over 2000 Covenanters were slain but Montrose lost only twenty-four men.

BAILLIESWELLS CRESCENT/DRIVE/ETC.

Bellis Wallis or Bellie's Wells is the site of March Stone No. 15. Nobody seems to know who "Bellie" was, and it has been suggested that the name merely means "small toun or farm". It was believed to be the haunt of elves and other spirits, and a herd boy there is said to have heard a mysterious voice which recited the verse:

"Bring me mattocks and bring me mells
Frae the box winnocks o' Bellie's Wells,
To dig down, to dig down".

This seems to support the legend that there was gold buried under the original boundary stone.

BALGOWNIE CRESCENT/ROAD/ETC.

From early times this was the name of the hamlet on the north end of the Bridge. The name Balgownie (or Polgown as it was sometimes called) means "town of the smith" or "smith's pool" and indicates that there was a blacksmith's forge at the hamlet. This would have been necessary because for centuries the Bridge was the only crossing place on the lower Don.

BANNERMAN PLACE

In the 15th century the Lands of Old Cruives, later the Estate of Woodside, were held by the Bannerman Family of Elsick, whose ancestors were standard-bearers to the Kings of Scotland.

BANNERMILL STREET

The Bannermill was a cotton factory, set up in the 1830's by a branch of the Bannerman family of Crimonmogate. It was sold about 1850 to Robinson, Crum and Co., and closed down in 1904.

BARBOUR BRAE

John Barbour (c.1316–1395). Archdeacon of Aberdeen and author of the great epic poem *The Brus*.

BARRON STREET

In 1756 Patrick Barron acquired the estate of Woodside and leased part of his lands for the setting up of a bleachfield and printfield. This was the origin of Gordon, Barron and Company, cotton manufacturers, whose Woodside Works at one time employed over 2000 hands. The business collapsed in 1850.

BATTOCK PLACE

In 1921 Baillie Wilson, Chairman of the Land Association, proposed that streets in the Torry district should be named after well-known hills visible from the area. Those chosen were Battock, Brimmond and Morven.

BEATTIE AVENUE/PLACE

James Beattie, poet and philosopher (1735–1803). Born in

Laurencekirk, he graduated from Marischal College in 1753 and became a teacher, first at Fordoun then at Aberdeen Grammar School. In 1760 he was appointed Professor of Moral Philosophy and Logic at Marischal College. In his youth he wrote poems about nature and contributed to the *Scots Magazine*. His collected poems appeared in 1761 as *Original poems and translations*, but he is best known for *The Minstrel*, a poem in which the hero finds his education in the woods and fields.

BEDE HOUSE COURT

The Bede House at Nos. 20 and 22 Don Street was the successor to Bishop Dunbar's Hospital, set up to house twelve poor men, each of whom had his own room and a little chimney. They had to be men of good conversation who had worked in the Cathedral precincts and as "bedesmen" they were expected to pray for the soul of the king.

BISHOPSLOCH ROW

Before the Bishop's Palace was built in the Chanonry, the Bishops of Aberdeen lived in their "manor-place on Lochgoul", so called because it was part of the estate of Goval. The remains of the Palace were found on the island there.

BLACKBURN PLACE

Bishop Peter Blackburn (died 1616). He was Bishop of Aberdeen from 1600 to 1616 and was the second Protestant bishop to hold office. He was reputed to be a miser and we are told "he was more mindful of a purse of merks than anything else". However, his "canniness" was probably born of necessity for Kennedy in his *Annals of Aberdeen* says that neither he nor his predecessor ever enjoyed any part of the Episcopal revenue, being contented with the small stipend which they received from the Magistrates as Parochial Clergymen.

BOOTH PLACE

Andrew G. Booth, Postmaster, (died 1954). Postmaster at Bucksburn from 1931 to 1953, Mr. Booth also represented the area on the County Council for 19 years. He was particularly interested in housing and during his term of office he saw the number of Council houses in the Bucksburn area increase from 100 to over 800. He was involved in several other organizations, both local and professional, and for a time was President of the Scottish Federation of Sub-Postmasters.

BORROWSTONE PLACE

The farm of Borrowstone was part of the estate of Bogfairley, feued to the Menzies family in 1551. Borrowstone came into the possession of the Weavers and Dyers Incorporation. The "doupin stane" on the property was used to initiate weavers into their trade.

BOYD ORR AVENUE/CLOSE

John Boyd Orr, 1st Baron Boyd Orr of Brechin (1880–1971). An expert on nutrition, he became Director of the Rowett Research Institute and Professor of Agriculture at Aberdeen, 1942–1945. He was first Director of the United Nations Food and Agriculture Organization and winner of the Nobel Peace Prize in 1949.

BRADLEY TERRACE

United States General Omar Nelson Bradley (1893–1981). He commanded the U.S. 2nd Corps in North Africa and took part in the invasion of Sicily. As Commander of the 12th Army Group he captured Cherbourg and moved on to cross the Rhine at Remagen.

BRIMMOND COURT/PLACE/VIEW

Brimmond or "Druman" Hill lies entirely within the Freedom Lands and the citizens had the right to cast peats from the Free Moss there. It was the site of a "fyir bitt" or beacon in the 17th century and in 1917 a memorial was erected on the summit to the men of the parish who fell in the 1914–18 war.

BROOKE CRESCENT

Sir Harry Brooke of Fairley (1846–1921). After serving for 15 years with the 2nd Battalion Gordon Highlanders, he devoted his time to the welfare of Gordon Highlanders and their dependants. One of his major achievements was the founding of the Gordon Highlanders' Institute.

BROOM PARK

This area was part of Mains of Cults, and the field on which it lies was always known as Broom Park.

BROOMHILL AVENUE/PARK/ETC.

The property of Broomhill is said to have been named by George Smith who acquired the land from the Duthies of Ruthrieston in the late 18th century. Broomhill House was demolished in 1937.

BROUGH PLACE

Robert Brough, A.R.S.A. (1872–1915). Born at Invergordon, he was apprenticed to a firm of lithographers in Aberdeen. He went on to study in Edinburgh and Paris and on his return to Aberdeen, spent three years as a portrait painter in the City. He then set up in a studio in London and his work was widely acclaimed. He became an A.R.S.A. in 1904 but less than a year later he was killed in a horrific railway accident.

BURNIEBOOZLE CRESCENT/PLACE

The lands of Burnieboozle consisted of the croft of Walker-hillock and parts of Springfield. It has been suggested that it was the name given to a stream which passed through Walker Dam and that it means "woody" or "bushy" burn from O.E. or Lowland Scots "boozie" or "bousy".

BYDAND PLACE

Bydand is the motto of the Gordon Highlanders and comes from the verb "bide" or "byde" meaning "wait" or "stand fast". A suggestion regarding the origin of the motto is given in *Lays of Strathbogie* by G.W. Anderson (1891). He says "To Jock of Scurdargue the Gordons are indebted for their motto. Word of some depredations on his lands having been brought to this fiery chief as he sat at meat, he sprang to his feet, jerking his dirk from its sheath. For several minutes he stood speechless, contemplating some terrible revenge, till, raising the weapon, he uttered the words "Byde and . . ." and struck his dirk into the table. After this the words "Byde and . . ." followed by a menacing gesture, were used by the Gordons to indicate that vengeance was in store".

BYRON AVENUE/CRESCENT/ETC.

George Gordon, 6th Lord Byron, poet (1788–1824). Many of the streets in this area are named from a Woodside connection and Byron is said to have lived for a short time at 177 Barron Street, the home of his nurse, Agnes Gray.

CADENHEAD PLACE/ROAD

William Cadenhead, poet (1819–1905). Working first in a thread factory in Carmelite Street, he later became an overseer at Broadford Works. His first published poem was *The Prophecy* set in the Vale of Seaton and in 1847 began his connection with the *Aberdeen Herald* and his friendship with fellow-poet and workmate William Anderson. The verses of both poets appeared regularly in the *Herald* from 1847–1853 and Cadenhead's poems were published in 1853 as *Flights of Fancy and Lays of Bon-Accord.*

CAIRNCRY AVENUE/CRESCENT/ETC.

Cairncry was part of the Freedom Lands, and was feued in 1764 by Sir Archibald Grant who laid out a fine park and erected a mansion house. The estate was famous for its granite quarries, 431 feet above sea level. G.M. Fraser suggests that the name derives from "Carn" (Cairn or heap of stones) and "Criach" (boundary) giving the meaning "Boundary Hill".

CAIRNFIELD PLACE (MILE-END)

This street was named in 1890, supposedly from Alexander Cairns who had a charter of the ground there.

CAPERSTOWN CRESCENT

Caprastoun was the name for Hilton before the estate was acquired by the Gordons of Pitlurg in the 18th century. It was sometimes written as Caponston or Capriston and is supposed to indicate the residence of a feuar called Capon or Caper.

CARDENS KNOWE

This is thought to have been the site of the Law Cairn where the Barony Courts were held. "Cathair" (seat or place); "Dain" (Judgement).

CARNIE DRIVE/GARDENS

William Carnie, writer and psalmodist, (1824–1908). Starting his working life as an engraver, he turned to journalism and in 1861 was appointed Treasurer of the Infirmary and the Asylum. His main interest was Church music and he was Precentor at the West Kirk, forming several successful choral groups. He published the *Northern Psalter* with great success in 1872. His three-volume work *Reporting Reminiscences* is a valuable account of Aberdeen's cultural and social life in the late 19th century.

CATTO CRESCENT/WALK

Mr. John Catto, farmer (died 1947). He became a member of Nigg Parish Council in 1931 and a District Councillor for the area three years later. He represented Nigg on Kincardine County Council from 1935 till his death on 14th February, 1947.

CATTOFIELD GARDENS/PLACE/TERRACE

The mansion house of this name was the residence of John Catto, a wealthy shipowner.

CHAPMAN PLACE/WALK/WAY

This commemorates the Chapman Road which ran from the croft of Oldtown to the Toll of Tyrebagger. It was part of the Via Regis or King's Highway which was the main road to the north until the 18th century, passing by Kittybrewster, Back Hilton Road, Oldtown, the Chapman Ford, Wagley and Ashtown.

CHEYNE ROAD

Henry Le Cheyne, Bishop of Aberdeen (died 1328). He was a nephew of John Comyn who was killed by Robert the Bruce in 1305. Boece says that he fled to England after the defeat of Comyn and that the rents which accumulated during his absence from his See went towards the building of the Brig o' Balgownie.

CLARKE STREET

Dr. John Clarke, Lecturer in Education (1853–1939). Born in Coleraine, Dr. Clarke was a graduate of Queen's

University, Belfast. After a spell in teaching, he was appointed headmaster of the Gymnasium, Old Aberdeen. Shortly afterwards he became a member of the Old Aberdeen Town Council and later served as Provost of the Burgh. He was appointed Lecturer in Education at Aberdeen University in 1898 and held the post till his retirement in 1925. He entered the Aberdeen Town Council as the member for St. Machar and represented the Ward till he retired in 1933. He was a keen sportsman and a successful golfer and mountaineer. He also played an important part in the formation of Aberdeen Football Club.

CLASHBOG PLACE

The Clashbog Well, Newhills, was famed for the coolness and purity of its water supply and was a regular stopping place for walkers on their way to Brimmond. The name means "Well at a ditch running from a marshy place".

CLERK-MAXWELL CRESCENT

James Clerk-Maxwell, physicist (1831–1879). He was Professor of Natural Philosophy at Marischal College at the age of 25 and his book *Electricity and Magnetism* opened the way to progress in this field.

CLOGHILL PLACE

Cloghill was part of the estate of Bogfairley, separately feued to John Dingwall about 1760. The oldest part of Cloghill House dates from 1771 and there was at one time a flint quarry on the estate.

CONINGHAM GARDENS/ROAD/TERRACE

Air Marshal Sir Arthur Coningham (1895–1948). He worked with the 8th Army in North Africa and formed the 1st Tactical Air Force, French North Africa in 1943. In 1944 he took command of the Tactical Air Force, N.W. Europe.

CORBY TERRACE

The Corby Loch lies in the north-west corner of Old Machar Parish. The name indicates that there were ravens there.

CORDYCE VIEW

The ridge of Cordyce or Tyrebagger divides the Parish of Dyce in two, rising to 824 feet on Caskieben and 763 feet on the Hill of Marcus. The higher part was a hunting forest but the lower slopes were cultivated from an early period. In 1316 Robert the Bruce gave Cordyce to Sir James Garviach, an ancestor of the Johnstons of Caskieben.

CORNHILL COURT/DRIVE/ETC.

Cornhill was part of the estate of Forresterhill till the 18th century when it was acquired by Alexander Thomson of Banchory. He sold it to Alexander Carnegie, the Town Clerk, and the last tenant was John Gordon, Assistant Burgh Surveyor. Tenders were invited for the demolition of the House and steading in May 1915.

CORTHAN CRESCENT/DRIVE/PLACE

"Corthan" is said to mean "a small stone circle", and though there seems to be no record of such a circle, Kincorth Hill was the site of numerous pre-historic monuments in the form of burial mounds, a cairn and a standing stone.

COVENANTERS DRIVE/ROW

The high ground of Kincorth was sometimes called Covenanters' Faulds because the forces of the Covenanters were encamped there on the 17th and 18th June 1639, prior to the Battle of the Bridge of Dee.

CRAIBSTONE AVENUE

The estate of Craibstone is first mentioned about 1330 under the name of Auchteronny. The first recorded owner, however, is John Crab, a Flemish engineer who had rendered valuable service to Robert the Bruce at the capture of Berwick. As a mark of his gratitude, the King gave him valuable properties including Auchteronny, which came to be referred to as Crab's town or farm.

CRAIGHAAR GABLES

Craighaar was the name given to part of the estate of Stoneywood. James Moir, the laird of Stoneywood, built a manor house there about 1683 and called it Stoneywood House.

CRAIGIEVAR CRESCENT/PLACE/ROAD

William Forbes, 1st Baronet of Craigievar (died 1648). A staunch Covenanter, he fought in Montrose's army at the Battle of the Bridge of Dee, 1639. He was ordered to secure deserters in Aberdeenshire in 1644 and was one of the Commissioners for selling "Malignants'" estates in 1646. He was appointed Sheriff of Aberdeen in 1647.

CROMBIE PLACE/ROAD

Crombie Road was named in 1893 probably in honour of John William Crombie who was Liberal M.P. for Kincardineshire 1892–1908.

CRUDEN CRESCENT/PARK/PLACE

Alexander Cruden (1701–1770). Born in Aberdeen, he set up as a bookseller in London. He is best known for his *Concordance of the Holy Scriptures,* first published in 1737. Plagued by bouts of insanity, he assumed the title of "Alexander the Corrector" and went round the countryside reproving Sabbath-breaking and profanity.

CRUICKSHANK CRESCENT (BUCKSBURN)

Dr. James Cruickshank (1869–1956). Born in Bankhead, he went to work at the age of 13 in the office of Messrs. Alexander Pirie & Sons of Stoneywood. He improved his position by reading and study and travelled overseas on behalf of the firm, eventually becoming Export Manager. He retired in 1922 and became local representative on the County Council Education Committee. He was Councillor for Newhills North from 1925 to 1956 and was regarded in his area as the final authority on such matters as employment, housing and education. He was County Convener from 1945 to 1949 and wrote several books and articles on the history of Newhills and the surrounding area.

CRUICKSHANK CRESCENT (KINCORTH)

Rev. Dr. Alexander Cruickshank, missionary in Calabar. (1854–1937). Born in Aberdeen, he was appointed in 1881 to Calabar where he served until 1937.

CUMMINGS PARK CIRCLE/CRESCENT/ETC.

The property of Cummings Park was formerly part of the Hilton estate and was purchased in the early 19th century by a Mr. Davidson of Kebbity who built the house and the steading. He was arrested for the murder of a servant girl there, but the Circuit Court returned a verdict of not proven. The estate was purchased by James Martin, tea planter from Ceylon and in the 1860's much ill-feeling arose over his decision to close off a right-of-way which led past his house. This resulted in an action and appeal in the Court of Session.

CUPARSTONE ROW

The Cappers-toun was a small community of "cappers" or makers of wooden cups. It was near to the Hardgate and the old road to the south and disappeared when Holburn Street was laid out in the early 19th century.

DALMAIK CRESCENT/TERRACE

This was the old name for the parish of Drumoak. It was

the Land or Field of St. Maik, otherwise St. Mazota, an Irish virgin to whom the Church of Drum was dedicated.

DALMUINZIE ROAD

Sir John Fleming's house at Murtle was called Dalmuinzie, this name having been given to it by its builder. An estate in Glenlochy has the same name probably because the land was owned by the MacIntoshes of Dalmuinzie in Perthshire.

DANESTONE CIRCLE/PLACE/TERRACE

This is a reminder of the conflict between the Scots and the Danes in the 9th century. A flat stone in Monument Wood, Grandhome is said to have been used as a writing table by the Danish Commander.

DAVIDSON DRIVE/GARDENS/PLACE

Provost Robert Davidson (died 1411). He is first mentioned in 1395 as Collector of the King's Customs. He was elected Alderman in 1405, and in 1411 he led the citizens at the Battle of Harlaw against Donald, Lord of the Isles and his Highland host. The citizens returned to Aberdeen bearing the body of their slain Provost and he was buried in Collison's Aisle in the Kirk of St. Nicholas.

DEANSLOCH CRESCENT/PLACE/TERRACE

This was an alternative name for the Bishop's Loch or Loch Goul. The palace of the early bishops of Aberdeen stood on an island there.

DEER ROAD

This was the road to the Deer Dyke which seems to have been part of the boundary between the estate of Woodside and the Lands of Cotton. It was sometimes called the Dirra Dyke or the Deir Dyke. It was probably a dyke made of sods to keep out the deer which abounded in this area.

DEMPSEY TERRACE

General Sir Miles Christopher Dempsey (1896–1969). He served in France and Italy and commanded the British 2nd Army in North-West Europe in 1944. In 1945 he was Commander of the 14th Army in Malaya.

DERBETH CRESCENT

The property of Derbeth was part of the estate of Bogfairley and was feued to Provost Alexander Aberdein in 1760. The name was made up from the final syallables of the Christian names of Alexan*der* and Eliza*beth* Aberdein.

DILL PLACE/ROAD

Field-Marshal Sir John Greer Dill (1881–1944). Chief of the Imperial General Staff in 1940–1941, he was sent to Washington as head of the British Joint Staff Mission. He was noted for his brilliance as a strategist and organizer.

DUGALD BAIRD COURT/SQUARE

Sir Dugald Baird (1899–). A world-famous obstetrician and gynaecologist, he was Regius Professor of Midwifery at Aberdeen, 1937–1965. He was made a Freeman of the City of Aberdeen in 1966.

EDMOND GARDENS

Dr. Francis Edmond of Kingswells (1805–1892). He qualified as an advocate in 1829 and as legal adviser to King's College he was the victor in a prolonged lawsuit concerning the Drum Bursaries. As a result he was given an L.L.D. Degree in 1881. He acquired the estate of Kingswells in 1854 and carried out improvements to the house and grounds. His name is associated with the building of the Consumption Dyke and the erection of Kingswells Church. On his death the estate was left as a Trust for benevolent purposes.

FAIRIES KNOWE

The mound of this name lies at the mouth of Fairley Den and is thought to have been a pre-historic cairn. It lies in the centre of the Freedom Lands so it was probably also the Law Cairn where justice was dispensed by the magistrates of Aberdeen.

FAIRLIE STREET

It is likely that this street was named after Rev. John Fairlie, who was Minister of Woodside Parish Church for 25 years. A native of Maybole, he came to Woodside in 1894. He was interested in everything which affected the community and was an active member of the School Board from 1897 to 1906. He died in 1920 at the age of 58.

FAULDS CRESCENT/GATE/ETC.

This comes from the name "Covenanters' Faulds" which was applied to the high ground at Kincorth in memory of the Covenanting army which was encamped there prior to the Battle of the Bridge of Dee in 1639.

FERGUS PLACE

It is believed that in earliest times Dyce was called "The Chapel of St. Fergus near Moss Fetach". St. Fergus was a Celtic saint of the 8th century, and the Old Church of Dyce is dedicated to him. In the Churchyard are the Dyce sculptured stones and a newer section contains the graves of Polish and Commonwealth airmen who died in World War II.

FETACH WALK

Moss Fetach was the name given to the low marshy ground lying between Nether Kirkton of Dyce and the river Don. The name comes from the Gaelic word "feithach" (marshy).

FERRIER CRESCENT/GARDENS

Sir David Ferrier, neurologist (1843–1925). Born in Woodside, he graduated from Aberdeen Univeristy in 1863. He continued his studies at Edinburgh and was appointed in 1889 to the specially created Chair of Neuro-pathology at King's College, London. He is best known for his books on the functions of the brain.

FINNAN BRAE/PLACE

The village of Seatown of Findon has long been famed for its smoked yellow haddocks, generally known as "Finnan" haddocks. The Barony of Fyndon or Finnan was held by the Chalmers family in the 14th century but by 1580 it had been acquired by Menzies of Pitfodels. In that year Alexander Menzies was ambushed and murdered while visiting the nest of a pair of falcons which were nesting on the rocks nearby.

FIRHILL PLACE

The Firhill Well stood in a lane behind the Snow Churchyard. It was said to be medicinal, but probably derived greater fame from the gingerbread or gibberie which was sold there by Baubie Courage and her assistant, two old ladies dressed in white aprons and mutches. The popularity of their wares gave rise to the alternative name "Gibberie Wallie". The Well has now been re-located in the Sunnybank sportsground.

FLOURMILL BRAE

The flourmill on the east side of St. Nicholas Street was driven by water power and was removed about 1865. For nearly thirty years after the Loch of Aberdeen was drained, the principal stream by which it had been fed continued to run from Loch street in an undergreound channel west of Drums Lane and across the Netherkirkgate.

FONTHILL ROAD/TERRACE

On 21st March 1892 the Town Council resolved that the name St. Machar's Place be abolished and the line of the street named Fonthill Road. G.M. Fraser was told that Fonthill House was built and named by Mr. Harvey Hall who was connected with the Farquhar family of Fonthill Abbey, Wiltshire.

FORRESTERHILL ROAD

The Lands of Forresterhill were part of the Freedom Lands and were feued to Gilbert Collison in 1551 for £20 Scots. The property was broken up in the late 18th century, the main divisions being Ashgrove, Woodhill, Stockethill, Cornhill and Westburn. The name is thought to come from the Foresters who were appointed as early as the 14th century to guard the Forest of Stocket.

FOWLER AVENUE

Dr. James E. Fowler, medical practitioner (1839–1915). A native of Skene, Dr. Fowler came to Woodside in 1865. His practice stretched from Dyce and Blackburn on one side and Nigg on the other, and for the next forty-five years he was a familiar figure as he travelled around, first on horseback, then in a gig and latterly in a motor car. Affectionately known as "Myrrh Jim", he was regarded in the area as a friend as well as a medical adviser. He arrived in Woodside just as it was beginning to recover from the depression caused by the closing of the Woodside Works and the Grandholm Mills and he soon became involved in the public life of the Burgh, serving as Chief Magistrate from 1871 to 1874.

FRASERFIELD GARDENS

The estate of Balgownie was known for a time as Fraserfield, the name having been adopted by William Fraser who purchased the estate in 1721. It was changed back to Balgownie by Mrs. Margaret Fraser Forbes who inherited the estate in 1808.

FRIENDSHIP TERRACE

Friendship Farm stood on the site now occupied by Ashley Road School. Its name was derived from a connection with Robert Balmanno, an 18th century Quaker or member of the Society of Friends who also gave his name to Mannofield and to his house which he called "Friendville".

FULLERTON COURT

John Fullerton, poet (1836–1904). Born at Woodside, he began work in the cotton mills at the age of ten. He attended evening classes at the Mechanics' Institute and obtained a post in a solicitor's office at Peterhead, later becoming Factor of the Pitfour estate. He contributed verses to newspapers and journals using the pseudonyms "Wild Rose", "Robin Goodfellow" and "Rip van Winkle". In 1870 his narrative poem *The Ghaist O' Dennilair* was issued as a booklet.

GAELIC LANE

This lies on the east side of Gaelic Chapel, founded in 1795 for the Gaelic-speaking congregation. The building was sold in 1882 to Messrs. G. & W. Fraser, printers.

GAIRN CIRCLE/CRESCENT/ETC.

One of the properties on the Lands of Countesswells was Le Garne, let to a certain John Anderson in 1398. It was later referred to as Gardin, Garden, Gardyne or Gairdyne.

GARDNER CRESCENT/DRIVE/ETC.

Alexander B. Gardner, City Architect (died 1961). He came to Aberdeen in 1924 as Director of Housing and Supervisor of the Town's Properties, and ten years later was designated City Architect. Among the buildings which he designed are the Bon-Accord Baths and the Rosemount flats, for which he was given a Saltire Society award. He was much involved with the development of the Kincorth estate.

GARTHDEE CRESCENT/DRIVE/ETC.

"Garth" is said to indicate that there was a weir on a river for catching fish. The estate of Garthdee was purchased from the Pitfodels Land Company in 1869 by Benjamin Moir and John Moir Clark, partners in John Moir & Sons, provision curers. They laid it out with fruit and vegetable gardens and turned Upper Kaimhill Farm into a piggery. An attempt to close off the new road to the Bridge of Dee in order to protect their produce led to an action in the Court of Session and they were ordered to remove all gates, fences and other obstructions. In 1953 Garthdee House was handed over to Robert Gordon's College by Councillor T. Scott Sutherland.

GARVOCK WYND

Laurence de Garvock, William Leith and John Crab were Aberdeen's first recorded Members of Parliament, being appointed Commissioners to the Scottish Parliament in 1357. Laurence de Garvock was appointed Alderman or Provost in 1366. He is thought to have been a son of Sir James Garvock of Balnacraig.

GILBERT ROAD

The land in this area belonged to the Seaton Estates and

the street name commemorates Gilbert Hay, elder son of James Gordon Hay of Seaton. He died of meningitis when less than two years old.

GILLAHILL PLACE/ROAD

The Lands of Gillahill were part of the Estate of Sheddocksley until the mid 18th century. The name is said to mean a "cattle fold" but some people connect it with "Gallow Hill", the place where hangings took place. On the farm is a small cemetery where the Resurrectionists are said to have buried their dismembered corpses.

GILLESPIE CRESCENT/PLACE

Lilias Gillespie, Quaker poetess (1626–1697). She was the wife of Baillie Alexander Skene of Newtyle. Her verses, written between 1665 and 1697 relate to her own spiritual experiences but also refer to the history of the Quakers at this time of persecution. Her son-in-law was Alexander Jaffray of Kingswells and she is buried beside her husband in the Quaker burial-ground there.

GORDON STREET

Thomas Gordon, a mason, had this street laid out in 1800–1807 and feued most of it for hand-loom weaving shops.

GORDON LENNOX CRESCENT

General Sir George C. Gordon Lennox (born 1908). After service with the Grenadier Guards and as Commander R.M.A. Sandhurst, he was appointed Colonel of the Gordon Highlanders in 1965. He retired in 1978, having successfully guided the Regiment through a time which had brought great changes to the British Army.

GORDONS MILLS CRESCENT/PLACE/ROAD

Gordon's Mills was the site of the first paper mill in Aberdeen, opened by Patrick Sandilands in 1696. By 1703 it was a textile mill and was referred to as "Northmills at Gordon's Mills". In 1703 the owner, William Black, petitioned Parliament to allow the levying of a tax for the maintenance of two apprentices from each Presbytery in Aberdeenshire at his mill, "the first of its kind set up in the nation". At this time it was producing a variety of cloths including broadcloths, drugget, serges, damask and plush made of wool.

GORT ROAD

Field-Marshal Viscount John Gort (1896–1946). Known for his bravery during World War I, he was appointed Chief of the Imperial General Staff in 1937. He commanded the B.E.F. in France and organized the defence of Gibraltar and of Malta.

GREAT WESTERN ROAD/PLACE/ETC.

The name was suggested by Mr. John Sutherland of Messrs. Edmonds & McQueen. The line of the road had several names and he suggested it because there was a road in Glasgow of that name with which Aberdeen Land Association was connected.

GREENBURN DRIVE/PARK/ETC.

These streets are named from the Greenburn which flows from Elrick Hill to the Don. Greenburn Road was part of the main road to the north from the 15th century until the opening of the Inverurie Turnpike Road in 1801. The Greenburn Markets were started by James Moir, Laird of Stoneywood, in 1701, and an Act of Parliament decreed that they should be held twice yearly on Hagg Fair and on Bathie Fair, i.e., the second Thursday in June and the last Thursday in July.

GREIG COURT

Councillor John A. Greig, (1905–1971). He worked for the Harbour Board for forty years and was elected to the Town Council in 1955 as the Representative for Mastrick. He served continuously till his death and acted as Housing Convener from 1964.

GROATS ROAD

Much of the land now occupied by the Hazlehead housing estate was reclaimed, single-handed, by a Mr. Groat. The owners of Backhill of Hazlehead in 1919 were James and William Groat.

HARROW ROAD

John Harrow, wigmaker (c.1709–1793). He bequeathed certain lands and houses in New and Old Aberdeen for the benefit of the poor. He owned Harrow's Croft and left it for a benevolent fund for Old Machar Church and Gilcomston Chapel of Ease.

HASMAN TERRACE

The Hasman is a rock just off the coast between Gregness and Souter Head.

HERMITAGE AVENUE

Powis Hermitage stood on a high knoll called the Firhill at the west end of Powis Lodge grounds. It was a three-storeyed brick building, roofed with thatch and surmounted by a crescent, the Fraser crest. Local legend claimed that it was the abode of a hermit who ventured forth at night through a secret underground passage to the sea-shore. The building was demolished in 1925.

HETHERWICK ROAD

Dr. Alexander Hetherwick, missionary (1860–1939). A farmer's son from Auchnagatt, he was licensed by the

Presbytery of Aberdeen in 1883 and was immediately appointed to the Blantyre Mission. He founded a Mission at Domasi and for many years he was an informal member of Nyasaland Legislative Council. He was the author of several books on African languages and on the work of the Church there.

HILTON AVENUE/COURT/ETC.

Formerly known as Capriston or Caperston, Hilton has always been admired for its fresh air and extensive views. Its situation made it an ideal site for a Bronze Age stone circle and it is thought that the Langstane, now in the grounds of Hilton Academy, is a survivor of that period. In 1561 the estate belonged to a William Watson and there were several changes of ownership before it was acquired by James Anderson in 1873. The estate was purchased by the Town Council in 1925 for a housing development at a cost of £22,000.

IRVINE PLACE

G.M. Fraser was told that the name comes from a contractor called Irvine, who had a house and a yard there. Another explanation is that Mr. Allan, the owner of the land, was married to an Irvine of Drum.

JOHNSTON GARDENS, CULTER

Kenneth J.C. Johnston, Housing Manager, (1931–1983). Born in Perth, Mr. Johnston came to Aberdeen in 1963 as Housing Manager for Aberdeen County Council. He was a pioneer in the provision of sheltered housing and was involved in the opening of Scotland's first such scheme at Merryvale, Dyce in 1966. He became ill in 1969, suffering from multiple sclerosis and his increasing disability forced him to resign in 1974. He died in Hillside Hospital, Perth on 11th December, 1983.

JOPP'S LANE

Provost James Jopp (1719–1791). He was a wine and cloth merchant and owner of the Lands of Cotton from 1776. He was Provost for three terms between 1766 and 1777 and these years are notable for the removal of two of the remaining "ports" of the burgh at the Gallowgate and Justice Street.

JUTE STREET

The Jute Works owned by the Aberdeen Jute Company, were situated nearby in Froghall Terrace. The company collapsed in the 1920's and the "Big Lum" was demolished on 4th June, 1935.

KEMP STREET

George Kemp, City Treasurer (1850–1914). A native of Aberdeen, he worked for thirty years with Messrs. J. Crombie and Sons, shipowners, before setting up his own office as an accountant in Bridge Street. He entered the Council in 1890 and represented first Rubislaw, then Rosemount. He was a Baillie and Convener of several Committees, becoming City Treasurer in 1911. Apart from his Council work, he was especially interested in the Temperance Movement and in Sunday Schools, and was a Governor of Robert Gordon's College. Over the years he built up an extensive collection of lantern slides of local views and landmarks, and these he bequeathed to the City Library.

KEPPLEHILLS DRIVE/ROAD

The Estate of Kepplehills or Capelhill was part of the Freedom Lands and was feued to William Forbes in 1579. The name is thought to come from its situation at the top of the rough, hilly ground leading up from the Chapel of

Stoneywood. Henry Forbes, the second of the family, changed its name to Newhills, the designation which was later adopted for the new Parish in 1666.

KETTOCK GARDENS

Kettocks Mills stood by the Don not far from the Brig o' Balgownie on the opposite bank from the Seaton estate. It was a grain grinding mill and later a flour mill. The legend of *The Goodwife of Kettocks Mills* relates the story of the miller's wife who was aroused from her tomb by the attentions of a grave-robber.

KINCORTH CIRCLE/CRESCENT/ETC.

G.M. Fraser believed that the name comes from the Gaelic "Ceann" (head or rough hill) and "Coirthe" (a standing stone). There seems to have been a standing stone on the south side of the hill but the whole area was rich in burial mounds and cairns and other prehistoric remains. The Lands of Kincorth and Craigshaw were purchased by the City from the Baker Incorporation in 1928 for £45,000.

KINGSWALK/KINGSWAY

These streets are close to the route of the Via Regis or King's Highway which was the main road to the north in the 14th and 15th centuries. It passed along what is now Clifton Road and proceeded south of the Dancing Cairns to cross the Bucks burn in the lower Howes heading for Wagley and Ashtown.

LADYWELL PLACE

The Lady Well stood on the east of St. Fittick's Church, and was reached from the road by a short flight of steps. A writer in 1903 suggests that it was the domestic well for the nearby manse and farm.

LANG STRACHT

This road used to be known as the Stocket Road or the Old Skene Road because until 1803 it ran all the way to Skene, passing through the policies of Kingswells House. It was displaced by the new Skene Road and Dr. Edmond of Kingswells had a small cottage built across it to prevent users from passing through his estate.

LANGSTANE PLACE

The "Lang-Stane" is thought to have been part of a Bronze Age Circle. Such circles were used by the Druids either as centres of worship or as burial places. Langstane Place would have been part of the old road which entered Aberdeen from the south, passing by the Hardgate and Windmill Brae to the Green.

LAWS DRIVE/ROAD

The Very Rev. Dr. Robert Laws, explorer and medical missionary (1851–1934). Apprenticed as a cabinet-maker in Aberdeen, he determined to take up missionary work and obtained an Arts Degree from Aberdeen. By the age of 25 he was on his way to Central Africa, facing danger and hardship in order to reach the Zambesi. He set up a mission at Cape MacLear, and at first the venture seemed a failure. In time, however, slavery was abolished and tribal wars ceased. In 1908 he became Moderator of the United Free Church and in 1928 he was given the Freedom of the City of Aberdeen.

LIDDEL PLACE

Duncan Liddel, mathematician and physician (1561–1613). Born in Aberdeen, he studied at King's College and on the Continent. He mortified the house and lands of Pitmedden Estate for the benefit of poor scholars in arts at Aberdeen University.

LOGIE AVENUE/GARDENS/ETC.

Francis Logie, a Quaker, was a proprietor of Upper Middlefield in the late 18th century. His daughter Ann married Alexander Pirie of Stoneywood Works.

LONGCAIRN GARDENS

The Long Cairn situated on the farm of West Hatton, dates from about 3000 BC and is thought to have been the burial place of a Stone Age Prince. When measured in the 18th century it was 108 feet long and 38 feet broad but it is now much broken down.

MACKAY ROAD

Alexander Murdoch MacKay, missionary (1849–1890). Born at Rhynie, he trained as an engineer, but turned to missionary work. He served in Uganda from 1878 until his death from malaria. In spite of opposition and bloodshed he made Uganda a centre for the evangelisation of Africa.

MAIDENCRAIG PLACE

The Lands of Maidencraig took their name from the legend of a Quaker girl who plunged to her death in the gorge there, following an unhappy love affair. The Mill of Maidencraig was built as a meal mill in 1616 to serve the northern part of the Freedom Lands and it was famous for its vast iron wheel which remained on the site till 1922.

MALCOLM ROAD, BUCKSBURN

This road was formerly called Damside, but the name was changed about 1916 in honour of Malcolm Vivian Hay, the Laird of Seaton. Major Hay served in the Gordon Highlanders, and his experiences are recalled in his book *Wounded and a Prisoner of War*. He also wrote several historical works of note.

MANOR AVENUE/DRIVE/ETC.

This name comes from the old Manor House of Middlefield.

MARCHBURN AVENUE/COURT/ETC.

The burn is the Scatterburn which was part of the boundary of the Freedom Lands. It also marked the City's boundary from 1891 to 1975.

MASTRICK DRIVE/ROAD/ETC.

G.M. Fraser believed that Provost John Ross of Arnage built a house here and named it after the town of Maastricht in the Netherlands where he had trading interests. Other writers suggest that the name is of Gaelic origin and means "a place where butter is churned".

MATTHEWS ROAD

Dr. Thomas T. Matthews, medical missionary (1842–1928). Born in Aberdeen he is generally known as "Matthews of Madagascar". He was ordained in the Free East Church in 1870 and immediately set out with his wife for Madagascar. For the next thirty years he was preacher, teacher and general adviser to the Malagasy and saw society changed due to the influence of an expanding Church. He translated several theological works into Malagasy and his experiences are described in his autobiography *Thirty Years in Madagascar.*

MENZIES ROAD

From the mid 16th century much of Nigg belonged to the Menzies family, while the Burgh of Aberdeen possessed the smaller remaining portion. In 1875 an agreement was reached whereby Aberdeen received all the land to the east of what is now Mansefield Road and the Menzies family retained the territory to the west.

MIDCHINGLE ROAD

This was the name given to fishings acquired by the Harbour Commissioners under the Harbour Act of 1871. They were river fishings as opposed to raik and stell which are sea fishings.

MOIR AVENUE/CRESCENT/ETC.

These streets were named after Mr. Alexander Moir, who was the farmer at Granitehill for 55 years.

MONTGOMERY ROAD

Field-Marshal Viscount Bernard Law Montgomery of Alamein (1887–1976). He commanded the British Eighth Army in Egypt and gained a crucial victory over Rommel's Forces at El Alamein. He commanded all the ground forces for the invasion of Normandy and was Deputy-Supreme Allied Commander, Europe, 1951–1958.

MONTROSE DRIVE

James Graham, Marquis of Montrose (1612–1650). At first a fervant Covenanter, Montrose led the army which occupied Aberdeen in March 1639. By June of the same year the City was in the hands of the Royalists and Montrose re-captured it at the Battle of the Bridge of Dee. By 1644, however, he had become an equally ardent supporter of the King and in the aftermath of the Battle of the Justice Mills he unleashed his "wild Irishes" on the City in a three-day orgy of murder, pillage and rape. Following his execution in 1650, one of his dismembered arms was displayed over the Justice Port.

MORGAN ROAD

Patrick Morgan, historian (died 1887). Born in Woodside, he served an apprenticeship at Gordon's Mills, later becoming an overseer in the spinning department at

Broadford Works. He was much involved in the work of the Free West Church and in the Temperance Movement. He is the author of *Annals of Woodside and Newhills* which is the main printed source for the history of these areas.

MORRISON DRIVE

Treasurer Alexander T. Morrison (died 1954). Entering the Town Council in 1931, he was Housing Convener from 1931 to 1935. He held the office of City Treasurer from 1935 to 1947 and during the war years was in charge of Civil Defence in the area.

MORTIMER DRIVE/PLACE

In the mid 17th century the Lands of Hisselheid or Hazelhead were acquired by Thomas Mortimer, a nephew of the Laird of Craigievar and one of Aberdeen's leading citizens. He was succeeded by his son Thomas, after which the estate passed to the Rose family in 1715.

MOSMAN PLACE

Thomas and William Mosman were proprietors of the estate of Middlefield in the 18th century. William Mosman was a well-known artist in Aberdeen and taught drawing to students of both universities.

MURRAY COURT

William Murray, flesher and farmer (c.1820–1891). Born in Woodside, he trained as a flesher and several years later he was at the head of an expanding business with connections all over Britain and in America. In 1861 he took a 19 year lease of the farm of Tipperty of Ellon which he farmed by advanced methods. He was respected for his generosity to the people of Woodside.

NEW PARK PLACE/ROAD

Until the 18th century, the property of New Park was part

of the Estate of Sheddocksley. It used to be called Cuttlehill, meaning "Hill of the cattle fold". In 1777 it came into the possession of the Dyce family and William Dyce, R.A. was born there in 1806.

OSCAR ROAD/PLACE

The Oscar was a whaling ship which was wrecked in Greyhope Bay on 1st April 1813. A storm arose while some of her crew were ashore and by the time she was ready to put to sea it was impossible for her to clear the Girdleness. She was driven on to the rocks and many of her crew were hurled from the rigging into the sea. There were only two survivors from the 44-man crew.

PERWINNES PATH

The Marish or Moss of Perwinnes was the name generally applied to the north part of Scotstown Moor, an area famed for the variety of its wild flowers. For several hundred years the Moor was part of the lands which belonged to the Bishopric of Aberdeen. Eventually the Bishops found it necessary to sell or to feu most of their territories, but the Moor was reserved as a Commonty for the use of the inhabitants of Old Aberdeen for pasture and peat. After the Reformation it became Crown property and survived for several centuries as a paradise for nature lovers. The 20th century, however, has brought hazards in the form of war-time cattle grazing, rubbish dumping and high density housing on its perimeters, and strenuous efforts by conservationists have failed to prevent its partial destruction.

PITDOURIE WALK

Pitdourie is thought to mean "place of the springs" from pit (place) and doubran (water). Pitdourie Well is a strong mineral spring on Tyrebagger Hill, near to the croft of the same name. It was a May-day wishing-well and people used to go there on the first day of May to drop a pin in the water and make a wish.

PITMEDDEN CRESCENT/ROAD/TERRACE

John Seton of Pitmedden had command of a detachment of Royalist troops at the Battle of the Bridge of Dee on 19th June 1639. While carrying the King's Standard he was shot through the heart with a cannon ball. Thus his descendants bear in the centre of their coat of arms a heart with drops of blood issuing from it.

PITTENGULLIES BRAE/CIRCLE

Pittengullies is said to mean "a farm in the fork between two burns". The farm-house of Pittengullies was once an inn on the Old Deeside Road.

PITTODRIE PLACE/STREET/ETC.

The name is said to derive from the Erskines of Pittodrie who had a property in the area. The estate of Pittodrie in the Garioch was formerly called Balhaggardie and was acquired by the Erskines in the 15th century. Pittodrie is thought to mean "the place of bleaching".

POLO GARDENS

The Polo Park is nearby and there the Piries of Stoneywood and their friends used to play polo. The park became a sports-field for Stoneywood Mill and was much used for community picnics and sports.

PORTAL CRESCENT/TERRACE

Charles Frederick Algernon, 1st Viscount Portal of Hungerford (1893–1971). Marshal of the Royal Air Force, he was Chief of Air Staff from 1940–1945. He was a member of the Combined Chiefs of Staff and played a major part in Allied Conferences.

PRINTFIELD TERRACE/WALK

Before it became a Police Burgh in 1868, the village of Woodside was known as The Printfield from the calico printing carried out at Woodside Works. Gordon, Barron and Company had its origins in a bleachfield and printfield set up on the estate of Woodside in 1775.

PROVOST FRASER DRIVE

Dr. Duncan Fraser, (1880–1966). Born in Nethybridge, he was apprenticed to the drapery trade and spent several years as a travelling salesman, eventually setting up his own business in Schoolhill. Aberdeen's first Socialist Lord Provost from 1947–1951, he was particularly interested in housing provision.

PROVOST GRAHAM AVENUE

Dr. John MacDonald Graham (1908–1982). Formerly Minister of Radnor Park Church, Clydebank, he was Professor of Systematic Theology at Aberdeen University from 1937 to 1971. He entered the Town Council as a Labour member in 1947, and served as Lord Provost for two terms, 1952–1955 and 1961–1964. He was much involved with the development of the Hazlehead Estate. Ill health forced him to resign from the Council in 1964.

PROVOST HOGG COURT

Dr. Norman Hogg (1907–1975). Born in Aberdeen and educated at Causewayend School, he worked as a baker with Messrs. Mitchell & Muil, later becoming full-time organizer for the Scottish Union of Confectionery and Bakery Workers. He was a member of Aberdeen Town Council for 23 years and Lord Provost 1964–1967.

PROVOST RUST DRIVE

Dr. James R. Rust (1873–1945). Born at Danestone, he was apprenticed as a granite cutter and became a partner in the firm of Rust and Alexander, (later Charles McDonald Ltd.). He served as a Parish Councillor for seven years and in 1914 he entered the Council as the Representative for Rosemount. He was noted for his business acumen and held several Convenerships including that of the Housing Committee. He was City Treasurer from 1920 to 1929 and negotiated the purchase of the estates of Hazlehead, Hilton and Kincorth. He served as Lord Provost from 1929 to 1932.

PROVOST WATT DRIVE

Dr. Edward W. Watt (1877–1955). On graduating from Aberdeen University he joined the staff of the *Free Press* of which his father was one of the proprietors. He became editor of the *Evening Gazette* and joint manager of Aberdeen Newspapers Ltd. in 1922. He was Lord Provost from 1935 to 1938 and during his term the Royal Infirmary buildings were opened by the Duke of York. He was specially interested in young people and was a leading figure in the Boys' Brigade.

RAMSAY CRESCENT/GARDENS/PLACE

At the Battle of the Bridge of Dee one of the few casualties on the Covenanting side was "a brave gentleman called Ramsay, brother to the Laird of Balmain". He was buried next day in the Kirk of St. Nicholas and his soldiers fired a dead volley at the Kirk door in salute.

REGENSBURG COURT

The Bavarian city of Regensburg has been twinned with Aberdeen since 1955 and numerous official and educational visits have been exchanged.

RICHMONDHILL COURT/GARDENS/ETC.

The name is thought to derive from Richmondhill, Virginia because the first proprietor made a fortune by buying up the last cargo of cotton to arrive in Glasgow before the outbreak of the American War of Independence.

RITCHIE PLACE

General Sir Neil M. Ritchie (1897–1983). Deputy Chief of Staff to Auchinleck in the Middle-East, he led the British 8th Army 1941–1942.

ROBERTSON SMITH COURT

William Robertson Smith, theologian (1846–1894). Born at Keig, he studied at Aberdeen, Edinburgh and on the Continent, and in 1870 took up a Professorship at the Free Church College, Aberdeen. His articles in *Encyclopaedia Britannica* brought a lengthy trial for alleged heresies and errors, and lost him his Chair. He became Editor-in-Chief of *Britannica* and contributed numerous articles to the 9th edition.

RORIE HALL

Dr. David Rorie, medico, poet and humourist (1867–1946). A well-loved doctor in Cults for nearly thirty years, Dr. Rorie was one of the outstanding personalities of the North-East. He produced several volumes of poems of which the best known is *The Lum Hat Wantin' the Croon*. His war service with the 51st Highland Division earned him the D.S.O. and the Legion of Honour and gave rise to a book of reminiscences called *A Medico's Luck in the War*.

ROSS CRESCENT

Provost John Ross of Arnage (1665–1714) is said to have acquired the Lands of Mastrick and built a house there.

ST. ANNE'S COURT

This is close to the site of the Lepers' Croft within which was the Lepers' Hospital and the Lepers' Chapel, built in 1519 and dedicated to St. Anne.

ST. RONAN'S CIRCLE/CRESCENT/ETC.

A house called St. Ronan's formerly occupied part of this site. St. Ronan was a Celtic saint who died about 778. Little is known of his life, but he is mentioned in the *Aberdeen Breviary* as a bishop of Kilmaronan in Lennox and is commemorated at several sites in Iona. Sir Walter Scott immortalised him in his novel *St. Ronan's Well.*

SANDILANDS DRIVE

The Lands of Cotton, later part of the Burgh of Woodside, belonged to the Sandilands family from about 1640 to 1748. They were related to the Sandilands of Craibstone, and Patrick, the second Sandilands proprietor of Cotton, was the first to introduce paper manufacture to Aberdeen.

SCLATTIE CIRCLE/CRESCENT/ETC.

Sclatie or Sclaty is said to come from the Gaelic "sleibhte" (a hill or hillside). It is the first recorded place-name in Newhills Parish for it is mentioned in 1136 as part of an endowment for St. Machar's Cathedral. Sclattie House was demolished about 1800 because the quarry was encroaching upon it, and the ruins were discovered when the quarry was being extended about 1925.

SHEDDOCKSLEY DRIVE/ROAD

The estate of Sheddocksley was part of the Freedom Lands and is first recorded in 1398. G.M. Fraser suggests that the name comes from that of an early feuar called Schethock, "lea" or "ley" being a pasture land. The estate was broken up into several separate feus but Sheddocksley itself is associated with the Young family. Sheddocksley House dated from the later 18th century.

SHEPHERD PLACE

Dr. James Shepherd, missionary (1847–1926). Born in Aberdeen, he served as a missionary at Udaipur, Rajputana, India. He became very influential among the hillmen and was awarded the two Kaiser-i-Hind medals.

SILLERTON LANE

On Paterson's map of 1746, the site of Robert Gordon's Hospital is marked as Silverton and for many years it was referred to locally as "Sillerton". There is doubt as to the reason for this but G.M. Fraser believed that Sillerton was Robert Gordon himself, and that he had an estate called Sillerton in Udny.

SINCLAIR PLACE/ROAD

David Sinclair of Loirston (c.1824–1911). Born in Cove, he became overseer then owner, of the farm of North Loirston. He later acquired the lands of Altens and Kirkhill and went to live in Loirston House. He worked hard for the community, being Chairman of the Parochial Board and the Parish Council, a County Councillor and Chairman of the School Board. He stood as a Conservative candidate in the Parliamentary Election of 1880.

SLESSOR DRIVE/ROAD

Mary Slessor of Calabar, missionary (1848–1915). Born in Mutton Brae, Aberdeen, she moved with her family to Dundee and became a "half-timer" in a linen factory. She determined to become a missionary and volunteered for service in West Africa, arriving in Calabar in 1875. For the next forty years she worked devotedly among the African people among whom whe was known as the "White Ma". Regarded as a missionary heroine, she was awarded the Order of St. John of Jerusalem in 1913.

SMITHYHAUGH ROAD

This was an old name for the Lands of Cruives or Old Cruives, so called from its proximity to the cruives or salmon traps on the river Don. The name of the estate was later changed to Woodside. The name Smithyhaugh would seem to indicate that there was once a smithy near the river.

SPADEMILL LANE/ROAD

A mill for turning the wooden handles of spades was in existence there before 1800. It stood on the south side of the Denburn, slightly east of Spademill Road. It was part of the photographic works of George Washington Wilson till 1890.

SPARK TERRACE

Mrs. Ruby Spark (died 1966). A former owner of the Cove Bay Hotel, Mrs. Spark served for thirteen years as the Representative for Nigg and District on Kincardine County Council and was responsible for many improvements in her area. She also worked for numerous public bodies including the Royal Workshops for the Blind.

SPRINGBANK PLACE/STREET/TERRACE

The property of Springbank was named from its owner Robert Spring, listed in the *Aberdeen Directory* of 1825/6 as a baker.

SUMMERFIELD PLACE/TERRACE

Summerfield House stood between Princes Street and the Broad Hill and was the property of a family called Symers or Summers in the early 19th century. There is a Sasine of 1838 in favour of the heirs of Charles Symers, gardener in Aberdeen, and the heirs were Elspet or Elsy Simmers, Janet Simmers and Christian Simmers or Ogg.

TANFIELD AVENUE/COURT/ETC.

Tanfield was part of the Lands of Cotton and took its name

in the mid 18th century from the occupation of its owner James Rait, who was a tanner. Tanfield was bought in 1797 by Alexander Shand, advocate, and he lived in Tanfield House at the top of Tanfield Walk, then called Shand's Walk.

TEDDER ROAD/STREET

Marshal of the Royal Air Force Arthur William Tedder, 1st Baron Tedder of Glenguin (1890–1967). He commanded the R.A.F. in the Middle East 1942–1943 and in January 1943 he was appointed C. in C. of the Mediterranean Air Command and co-ordinated the Allied drive through Tunisia, Sicily and Italy. He was Eisenhower's Deputy Commander for the Normandy landings.

TILLYDRONE AVENUE/COURT/ROAD

G.M. Fraser suggests the name means "thorny hillock" from the Gaelic "tulach" (hillock) and "draigheann" (thorn). The name is applied to the "Motte" of Tillydrone, a conical grassy hillock overlooking the Don. From its commanding position overlooking the river crossing and the highway to the north, it is thought to have been the stronghold of some Celtic chieftain.

TOLLOHILL CRESCENT/DRIVE/ETC.

On the 17th June 1639 the army of the Covenanters gathered at Tollohill overlooking the Bridge of Dee. There they camped for two nights and from there they launched their successful attack on the bridge on the 19th June.

TWO MILE CROSS

This was a landmark on the Old Deeside Road near Garthdee Farm. We are told that the citizens marched out to meet Montrose's army there on 11th September 1644. They returned to the town the next day and their place at the Two Mile Cross was taken over by the enemy who camped there on the eve of the Battle of the Justice Mills. There was a farm called Two Mile Cross but it was merged in the property of Garthdee in the mid 19th century.

URQUHART LANE/PLACE/ETC.

Baillie Robert Urquhart (c. 1811–1877). Born in Midmar, he set up in business as a tea merchant. In the 1860's he became first a Police Commissioner, then a Town Councillor. He was on the Board of Management of the Royal Infirmary, the Lunatic Asylum and the Mechanics' Institute and was much interested in schemes for the housing of the working classes.

WAGLEY COURT/PARADE/PLACE

This is thought to come from the Old English word "waggle", meaning marsh or bog. Certainly there was marshy ground there, for the marsh gases gave rise to a "Will o' the Wisp", referred to as "The loupin lichts o' Wagley".

WATCHMAN BRAE

In 1627 there was a threat of a Spanish invasion and Brimmond Hill was selected as the site of a "fyir bitt", a beacon which would alert the countryside of the approach of the enemy. The croft of Watchmanbrae was the dwelling place of the keeper of the beacon who was to light up as soon as he saw the glow of the first "fyir bitt" on Castle Hill.

WAULKMILL CRESCENT/ROAD

In a waulkmill, cloth was thickened or felted by processes of soaking, beating and scouring. There seems to have been a waulkmill on the Lands of Cruives or Woodside in the mid 17th century for it is mentioned in various charters of the time. It was later converted into a copper mill and by the mid 18th century it was being used for the manufacture of snuff.

WAVELL CRESCENT

Field-Marshal Archibald Percival Wavell, 1st Earl Wavell (1883–1950). He was Commander-in-Chief Middle East 1939–1941, and drove the Italians from Cyrenaica and Ethiopia. He was appointed Commander-in-Chief India in 1941 and succeeded to the Viceroyship in 1943. He was a Chancellor of Aberdeen University.

WEBSTER ROAD

Rev. Dr. James Webster, missionary in Manchuria (1854–1923). Born in Auchintoul, Banffshire, he was educated at Aberdeen Grammar School and Glasgow University. He was chosen to go to Manchuria with Dr. Dugald Christie in 1882 and in spite of many difficulties, he won the confidence of the Chinese people. He was responsible for the organization and working of the Red Cross in the Russo–Japanese War.

WILKIE AVENUE

Baillie Alexander Wilkie (1854–1927). Born near Alford, he was apprenticed as a photographer to George Washington Wilson, eventually setting up his own business in Woodside. He became a Police Commissioner in Woodside and helped to promote its merger with Aberdeen. As Convener of the Links and Parks Committee, he organized the building of the Beach Promenades and the Bathing Station. He became immensely interested in public transport and from 1898 to 1902 he was Convener of the Tramways Committee and directed the electrification of the tramway system. In 1911 he left the Council and devoted his attention to the Suburban Tramway Company.

WINGATE PLACE/ROAD

Major-General Orde Charles Wingate (1903–1944). A master of unconventional warfare, he conducted the irregular campaign in Ethiopia and in 1943 he led the Chindits on a six-week foray behind the Japanese lines in Burma. He was killed in an air crash while leading a second mission.

INDEX OF STREET NAMES